AGAINST FATE

Loyola Lecture Series in Political Analysis

Richard Shelley Hartigan
Editor and Director

AGAINST FATE

An Essay on Personal Dignity

Glenn Tinder

University of Notre Dame Press
Notre Dame, Indiana 46556

Manufactured in the United States of America

Paperback edition 1984

Library of Congress Cataloging in Publication Data

Tinder, Glenn E.
    Against fate.

    (Loyola University series in political analysis)
    Includes bibliographical references.
    1. Fate and fatalism.   2. History—Philosophy.
3. Political science.   I. Title.   II. Series.
BJ1461.T5   170   81-50462
ISBN 0-268-00595-8   AACR2
ISBN 0-268-00607-5 (paper)

FOR GLORIA

Not the intense moment
Isolated, with no before and after,
But a lifetime burning in every moment
And not the lifetime of one man only
But of old stones that cannot be deciphered

T. S. Eliot
Four Quartets

CONTENTS

SERIES EDITOR'S PREFACE

THE CLOSING DECADES of the twentieth century pose situations and problems new to the human race: nuclear energy, overpopulation, dwindling resources of every kind, genetic engineering, and irreversible ecological damage. We are also witnesses to continued racial hatred, political instability, and ideological confrontation. These latter problems are not new.

New or old, what they share in common is that they must be addressed by political philosophers. Since Socrates, who first demanded that we assume responsibility for our acts rather than blame the gods, western philosophy has assumed the burden of attempting to define and understand the creature who we call a political animal. It may be a measure of our species' complexity or of our ignorance, or both, which accounts for the fact that we have yet to agree on a definition of what man is and what he should be. Nevertheless, the speculation must continue.

In 1968 Loyola University of Chicago instituted the Loyola Lectures in Political Analysis. The intent was to provide a needed forum in which political philosophers could express their views to a critical audience and then have the opportunity to revise and elaborate their ideas in a subsequent book. The Lecture Series has established itself as the vehicle for which it was intended, and it has done so largely because of the cooperation of its participants.

It was most appropriate that Glen Tinder should deliver the sixth presentation of the Loyola Lectures. His widely used book, *Political Thinking*, has become a standard text in classrooms where the perennial questions about man's nature and behavior are debated. The present work will complement his previous analysis of man's nature, drives, and desires. But even more valuable than his scholarly attention to man and his problems in the waning of the twentieth century was the personal attention which he gave to the faculty and students of Loyola University during his stay. I, and all associated with the Lecture Series, are deeply grateful for his efforts to communicate to us the fact that human problems can be solved by humans.

Richard Shelley Hartigan

ACKNOWLEDGMENTS

A NUMBER OF PEOPLE have helped me greatly in writing this essay.

No one did more than my good friend Jack Beatty, of *The New Republic*. Jack not only read and usefully criticized an early draft, but his conversation constituted the matrix of the essay. The combination of personal friendship and intellectual attentiveness which he provided at the time I was developing the ideas of fate and destiny was invaluable.

Three friends on university faculties read a late version of the manuscript. These were Professors Clarke Cochran of Texas Tech, Wally Meade of Illinois State, and John Nelson of the University of Iowa. Each supplied carefully worked-out critiques, along with encouragement, which helped immensely in bringing the manuscript to completion.

In addition, I wish to thank Loyola University of Chicago for inviting me to present the manuscript in lecture form through the annual Loyola Lectures in Political Analysis. As a way of trying out the main ideas in the essay, delivering those lectures was a unique and stimulating opportunity. In particular I wish to thank three political theorists and friends at Loyola University—Professors Tom Engeman, Dick Hartigan, and Jim Wiser—for their warm hospitality and their intellectual companionship during the period of the lectures.

Finally, I wish to mention my son, Galen Tinder, who in the case of this book as in that of others I have written, helped at critical points to uphold my morale by finding ideas I had worked out, but felt very unsure of, plausible and even, now and then, true.

PROLOGUE

MY MAIN CONCERN in the following pages is with what is now usually called "the dignity of the individual," or, in the terminology of Immanuel Kant, with the quality by virtue of which every person should be treated as an end and never merely as a means. This I believe to be the primary intuition of Western moral consciousness and indispensable to polities of the kind that recognize the needs and rights of every human being. My concern with this concept stems from my conviction that it is not only important but is being lost. It is a deeply mysterious idea. How can it be said that someone ruined in body, mind, and character bears an inviolable dignity? It is, moreover, necessarily in tension with political, economic, and administrative practice, which involves strong pressures to treat every individual simply as a calculable and expendable resource. Hence it is not surprising that it has been terribly and extensively violated in times as troubled as ours and that it seems often to be little more than a cliché of popular rhetoric.

"Fate" I use as a term to designate all that assaults personal dignity. Fate is the impersonal and the antipersonal, pervading time and space—determining events, and shaping society so comprehensively that there is no escape. Fate is present in all historical eras, but it is more dominant in some eras than in others. We live today, I believe, in unusually fateful times.

To withstand fate, we must find ways of reaffirming the dignity of the single person. The concept of destiny is employed to this end. In common usage, destiny is often equated with fate. Occasionally, however, the term is used

1

to suggest that destiny, even if preordained and severe, is somehow congruent with humanity in a way that fate is not. It is sometimes suggested, for example, that we may fail to measure up to our destinies. This never would be said of fate. I shall try to widen and exploit this distinction. I hope in this way to bring to the support of the individual human being some of the mystery and power evoked by the concept of destiny. In short, I shall set destiny in opposition to fate. I shall do this by construing as destiny the mysterious quality that renders every individual an end and not merely a means.

This is to speak very generally. Let me try to be more specific. The goal of this essay is to use the concepts of fate and destiny to illuminate the present historical situation. If these concepts work as intended, they will help us see how personal dignity is threatened and how it may be defended. Readers must be warned that so broad a goal means neglecting details, even rather large and important details sometimes, in order to try to see and identify the configurations of the whole. I try relentlessly, even if not always successfully, to look at things comprehensively. This means that in interpreting our present historical situation I block out an interpretation of history in general. In short, I try to construe our circumstances with philosophic breadth and this requires placing them in the context of a philosophy of history, or at least of a sketch of a philosophy of history.

This may sound intolerably presumptuous. One excuse I would offer is that we have little choice. We are forced to try to understand our situation as a whole because we are forced to live in that situation as a whole. We must philosophize about history because we must live within history. Specialization is the luxurious duty of scholars but is not permitted us as (in Kierkegaard's phrase) "existing individuals." The folly of attempting to take in everything at a glance is properly eschewed by scholars in their capacity as scholars. If eschewed by all of us, however, it would indicate that we had forgotten that we are concrete human beings with the task of living life as a whole. If both the scholarly folly and human necessity of the task are kept in mind, perhaps it can be undertaken without arrogance.

Another excuse I would offer for embarking on so large an undertaking is that I do not try, in a fundamental way, to be original. I try merely to make in a new way certain points that are very old. These old points are Christian. My views of personal dignity and of history are Christian, although my arguments are presented on grounds of reason and not of faith. Indeed, I would have little confidence in the ideas I present if they were drawn merely from my own mind rather than from Christian traditions. What is original lies in the concepts employed. I have cast the Christian view of human beings and history in novel terms. In this way I hope to make it possible for a vision that is profound and ancient, but unacceptable to many in our day, to illuminate our times.

At the core of my argument is the idea that fate is ironical: although it seems to come upon us from without, the truth is that we ourselves are the authors of our fate. Swept up in a drive to master the natural and social worlds, and ignoring the finitude and imperfection of man, we encounter human limits suddenly and disastrously. Fate is made up of the unexpected consequences of our own actions.

At present we are on the crest of a wave that is already breaking. The drive to mastery is evident in technology, revolution, and the prevalence of ideologies. I try to show how, as a consequence, nature, society, and history all have taken on fated qualities. Looking on nature as nothing more than material to serve human convenience and avarice, for example, we have lost the sense, expressed in both Hebraic scripture and Greek philosophy, of the underlying harmony of humanity and nature; results are evident in the noxious and unsightly environment so often created by modern industry. Striving forcibly and swiftly to reshape society according to the (perfectly valid) ideals of liberty, equality, and fraternity, we find ourselves in an era of bureaucracy and totalitarianism. In our determination to direct the course of history, we have lost our very consciousness of historical continuity; both past and future confront us as fate. All of this, I try to show, is ironical but not accidental. It originates in our pride—a pride evident not among radicals alone but also in various ways among liberals and conservatives.

The fatefulness of our times is deeply hostile to personal dignity. This hostility is sometimes subtle and beguiling, as when capitalist societies tempt their members to live for the sake of physical comfort. It is sometimes violent and frightening, as in the widespread use of political torture. In all of its forms, however, fate challenges us to reaffirm and defend personal dignity. To this end we must understand personal dignity, and I attempt to show how this can be done by means of the concept of destiny.

Here again, however, we encounter something disruptive of the drive to mastery. Destiny, like fate, is ironical and is not made according to human will and desire. The irony of destiny is that even though it is the intimate and sacred self, it is given to us—not as a natural necessity but as a personal possibility and a moral demand. Our dignity consists in our possession of destinies and is affirmed through fidelity to our destinies.

Our situation is thus that in our technological and revolutionary pride we have lost our sense of destiny and have fallen under the dominion of fate. Yet there are possibilities of renewal. Fate is something we have made, not simply suffered, and destiny continues to be demanded of us. The possibilities of renewal, moreover, are not just for individuals but for all of us together. Although destiny is personal, it is also universally human and becomes accessible only as we recognize our responsibility for the common life of humanity—a life that links generations in history. We need today, in place of the crumbling idea of progress, a reawakened consciousness of destiny as the ordained form of our common life in time. To be open to and to act upon the demands of universal destiny is "the true political art"— a phrase Plato applied to Socrates' conduct of his own life and the title of my final chapter. While only the final chapter deals explicitly with this art, I would like to think that the entire essay elucidates its nature and requirements. Although my view of our immediate situation is pessimistic, my view of the human situation altogether is very far—as must be so with any Christian—from despairing.

Chapter 1 is devoted to the concept of fate, chapter 2 to that of destiny. I cannot, however, postpone all discussion of destiny to chapter 2. The concept of destiny is at least partially presupposed by that of fate and it plays a central and unique role in the essay as a whole. This makes it desirable for the reader to gain a preliminary understanding of the meaning I assign to the concept.

THE CONCEPT OF DESTINY

Destiny is selfhood. It is, however, selfhood of more than an ordinary, observable kind. To gain an initial idea of what kind of selfhood it is, the concept of soul may be useful. To say that a human being has a destiny may be taken to mean roughly what has often been meant by saying that a human being has a soul. At the same time, the concept of destiny has connotations that the concept of soul does not have and that the conditions of our time render important. The following comparisons may clarify these statements.

(1) Destiny, like the soul, is the true, authentic self. The distinction between the essential and the merely accidental self goes back to ancient times and persists to the present day. It is implicit even in Freud, in spite of his skeptical and irreligious temper, and in the customary usage of those (often agnostics or atheists) concerned with the problem of identity, of "finding out who you really are."

(2) Destiny, like soul, designates a self that is transcendent in the sense of not being simply a thing in the world. It is not usually thought of as directly and comprehensively observable or as scientifically knowable, although observation or scientific knowledge might contribute to its being realized— through psychoanalysis, for example. The concept of a

transcendent entity is apt to arouse misgivings in this skeptical age, yet again and again we acknowledge the mystery, the inviolable inwardness, of personal being.

(3) A person's destiny, or soul, is sacred. It is the self to which, for Shakespeare's Polonius, one ought above all to be true; it would profit one nothing to gain the whole world and lose that self. The doubts of the present age have become so profound that the very category of the sacred has become questionable. Nevertheless, we cling to the notion that every individual is of infinite value and must be treated as an end, not merely a means.

It may seem that putting an unfamiliar word in place of a familiar one is likely to produce confusion. But when the old word has become trite and worn and we yet feel a need to speak of what the old word referred to, then trying a new term is surely in order. This would seem particularly so if what we are trying to speak of is profoundly important.

The concept of destiny, then, may help us to keep in view a reality it might be catastrophic to forget. It is not merely its novelty, however, that may render it useful. The concept of destiny has some advantages over that of the soul.

(1) The self is not so likely to be taken for an observable, controllable thing when it is spoken of as a destiny as when it is spoken of as a soul. To attribute a destiny to someone is quite unmistakably to acknowledge a mystery, and this perhaps has importance in an age when the sanctuaries of personal being are repeatedly violated by objectifying statisticians, bureaucrats, and technicians.

(2) A destiny cannot be thought of as a completed and established reality, as can a soul. Rather destiny is a demand, or an imperative. If we are thinking in terms of destiny we shall be disinclined to accord unquestioned authority either to the established conventions or to the intellectual abstractions that often stifle authentic selfhood.

(3) A destiny is a demand coming from beyond one's immediate environment and even from beyond the world as a whole. This is indicated by the impression of cosmic unconditionality that the term conveys. To try to live according to

a destiny is to resist the slovenly reduction of life to comfort and expediency that is encouraged by commercial and popular culture.

(4) As a demand, a destiny encounters resistance—realities and conditions that are not destiny but mere brute and impersonal matters of fact. We look for a term to designate these realities. The concept of soul has no counter-concept, although anyone willing to use the term at all would acknowledge that a soul encounters much that is not soul. The concept of destiny does have a counter-concept: that of fate. We shall try in the following reflections to avail ourselves of the advantages this duality of concepts offers.

(5) Finally, although destiny encounters fate, it is not— so the concept implies—hopelessly in conflict with reality. To speak of someone's destiny is to speak of that which *must*, in spite of all that is fateful and resistant, somehow come to fruition. This is true even if someone's destiny is tragic, for we may speak of a tragic (although certainly not of a disastrous, or catastrophic) fulfillment. Those employing the concept of soul have ordinarily assumed some such cosmic harmony, but the concept itself does not imply that harmony. The concept of destiny, in short, has greater intrinsic metaphysical weight.

Numerous intuitions give color and substance to the concept of destiny. These will be brought out in the course of the discussion.

The concept of destiny provides common ground for spiritual discourse—ground open to all, regardless of religious attitudes. The main ideas of this essay are interpretations of Christian wisdom, reflecting my own Christian faith. But to speak of Christian *wisdom* is to speak of insights which have been drawn from Christian faith but which one does not have to be a Christian to understand and accept. If Christ is the Logos, Christian faith and Christian wisdom are not indissolubly linked. I believe that the concept of destiny— spoken of in various ways—is simultaneously at the center of Christianity and an intuition and idea available to human beings of every persuasion. It can therefore enable people who are of varying religious faiths or even of no faith at all to inquire together into spiritual matters. For us to do that, particularly as spiritual matters impinge on political matters—in sum, for us to reflect together on the relations of the realm of spirit and the realm of Caesar—seems to me as urgent as any intellectual task before us.

1

FATE

FATE IS ALL THAT threatens and befalls us. It comes upon us from without, often strange and uninvited, always at enmity with personal being. In words made commonplace by our familiarity with fate, it is "meaningless" or "absurd." Fate may be fragmented and appear in the form of disjointed circumstances, or it may be massive and unified, even predictable. It may be experienced in recurrent jolts or in situations that devour us. It is always alien and dangerous.

To speak more precisely, fate is history of a certain kind. It is history that is antipersonal, irresistible, and inescapable. Persons are threatened in their personal distinctness, as by the inducements of advertisers, or in their very lives; they cannot alter the circumstances around them or direct the course of affairs; and wherever they go—to a city, to a small town—they still are threatened.

Fate is felt in different ways in different historical times. In some it is experienced as the reign of chaos and chance, in others as an inhuman predetermination of events. The latter—history experienced as vast, monolithic, and overwhelming—is what we often mean by fate, and it provides the more accurate impression. Accident, of course, always enters into an encounter with fate. That *I* should be one of those struck by a war, an accident, a plague, is never wholly explicable in terms of general conditions. Nonetheless, general conditions hold sway more extensively than a victim of

9

fate usually realizes. My personal plight can always be placed in a societal context and a causal order.

Societal and causal interconnections make an event rationally comprehensible but not "meaningful." The meaning people long for (and demand so persistently that the words they use in doing this have become trite) is found finally only in what contributes to sustaining or enhancing personal being. Even suffering and death can gain meaning in this way—if, for example, undergone as a just punishment or accepted in an act of deliberate sacrifice. Anything unrelated or hostile to personal being, however, is meaningless even if linked in an intelligible chain reaching back to the beginning of time. This is illustrated in twentieth-century experience. Many of the events and realities of our age have seemed "absurd," yet our history appears massive, unified, and predetermined. The absurd presents itself as "world-historical."

While fate is always alien and dangerous, however, it is not always unpleasant. Industrial society has provided an enjoyable fate for many in Western Europe and America. It has bestowed on vast numbers of people comforts and distractions that kings could not enjoy a few centuries ago. But these are fateful pleasures. They divert us from the tasks of selfhood more beguilingly, but not less effectively, than the atrocious conditions imposed on the working classes early in the industrial revolution.

In the twentieth century we have been overwhelmed by fate. Wars, revolutions, economic breakdowns, and other sweeping disasters have occurred. Also, a cascade of unexpected and unwilled pleasures, conveniences, impressions, and opportunities has come down upon many of us. Distant and uncontrollable powers determine how we shall live and die. A major experience for almost everyone is that our lives, whether terrible or agreeable, are decided upon elsewhere.

A symptom of our plight is the appeal held for us in the unassuming phrase "human scale." The powers and organizations that govern us, the realities that make up our world, are too vast. Every person is overshadowed by corporations and bureaucracies, superpowers, human multitudes, unimaginably destructive weapons. We cannot experience these things as we do trees or houses or anything else with definite and perceptible proportions. We can hardly even conceive of them, although we know well enough that they are real. Anyone undeluded by power or pleasure feels small, in fact negligible, both in value and influence.

It is not only the size of these monstrous realities that disturbs us, however, but also their apparent autonomy. They are seemingly out of control. Our future is not our own. Yet to say that the great powers of the world are out of control does not mean merely that they are out of your control and mine. We sense that they are not controlled by anyone. We are told occasionally that some kind of elite—business executives or bureaucrats, for example—rules us. Society is depicted in the lurid colors of conspiracy. Although analyses of this kind often purport to be alarming, they are in fact strangely consoling. They make the world seem relatively human and comprehensible.

Such consolation is probably illusory. Elites today probably effect no purposes more distant and sweeping than the expansion of their own wealth and prestige. Elitist theories, however, do contain a glimmering of truth. Fate is a human product. This is manifest. The vast events and powers that overshadow our lives have been created by humanity itself. Wars, economic dislocations, bureaucracies, tyrannies: all are human products. Fate is thus ironical. Although it is something that befalls us, it is also something that we ourselves have brought into being. It is not surprising, of course, that people should bring harm on themselves. What is surprising is that they should persistently experience this harm as having struck them from without.

The irony of fate, surprising at first glance, has been apparent to the greatest analysts of fate in our time. For Marx, it might be said, fate was embodied in capital, and capital was created by the very working class it oppressed. Capital was the worker's alien self. The capitalists were not independent conspirators but, like the workers, although more pleasurably, victims. Freud, too, was a student of fate. The founder of psychoanalysis gave his attention primarily to the instinctual drives denied satisfaction, in some cases necessarily, by organized society. Pressing for satisfaction in secret and circuitous ways, these became the fate not only of neurotic individuals but of civilization as a whole. For Marx and Freud both, fate was estranged humanity: labor power or erotic passion set against its original possessors.

Do not the ruling classes, however, bear a special responsibility for this inner enmity that curses modern society? Is elitism really false? The most serious weakness in elitist theory is its dependence on implausible assumptions concerning the relationship of human beings to the social order. The multitudes are necessarily seen as either forced or fooled into supporting the social order. But it cannot be that they are forced. Vast and durable historical realities cannot exist without widespread and spontaneous support. Force can stifle the opposition of minorities but not that of whole populations. To suppose that the brute facts of our fate depend on force is unduly to flatter force. It is also to underestimate the docility of most people and the power of the seductions deployed by advanced industrial society. Marx was guilty of these errors in forecasting the rise of a revolutionary proletariat. Marx's expectations have been repeatedly compared with present realities. In this way social commentary has underscored the submissiveness of peoples.

Are populations then seduced or fooled into supporting unjust and oppressive arrangements? To hold that they are is to ignore the shrewdness of ordinary human beings; you cannot, as Lincoln noted, fool all of the people all of the time. When people are fooled by political leaders or seduced by advertisers, it is because at bottom they are willing for this to happen.

Elitist theory not only unrealistically depreciates the many; it also unrealistically exalts the few. It cannot avoid assuming that ruling minorities stand entirely above the social order and its moral beliefs, cynically using these for their own advantage. Few people of power, however, are so cold and calculating. Most of them cannot use their power decisively and steadily without believing in what they are doing. If they believe in what they are doing, then they too are victims of fate, although victims of a different and perhaps more unattractive sort than those they rule and exploit.

Elitism may of course be qualified to meet these objections, but insofar as it is, it loses the characteristic attributes of elitist theory. No doubt there are many differences in life and character between rulers and ruled. But the majority is not made up mainly of slaves or fools and the powerful are not simply clear-eyed and selfish cynics. On both sides there is unfeigned allegiance to the beliefs and ways that shape our fate.

It is fair to say, then, that almost everyone—with varying motives and degrees of enthusiasm, related often to class and power—bears not only fate but some responsibility for creating fate. Our historical circumstances sometimes look like the handiwork of a malign and unknown god. But in actuality they are products of our own designs and actions.

Fate is brutal factuality, and our world is fated because it is dominated by powers that are wantonly inconsiderate of the core of our humanity, the distinct personality. How uncanny, then that these brutal facts are human. Again and again it is said that the world today is inhuman. It is true that our world is inhuman in its indifference to personal well-being and integrity. But in its origins, its structure, and its energies it is pervasively and manifestly human. Never before has the world been so human. The environment for most of us is almost completely a human artifact, or conglomeration of human artifacts, and enclaves of nature survive only with determined protection. The most fateful events of our time have not been earthquakes and droughts but revolutions and wars, movements that sweep over the earth like plagues but are purely, if devastatingly, human.

The "inhumanity" of our world is ironical not only because of its actual human source and character but also because of the immense self-confidence of recent generations.

The explorers, scientists, settlers, revolutionaries, and industrialists who drew the outlines of our fate were not diffident and hesitating people. Most of them were carried by a tidal wave of faith in human power and intelligence. Our dismay in the twentieth century, contemplating our times, is in ironic contrast with the exuberance of our predecessors.

Many have found an explanation for our misfortunes in our individualism. Our mistake, it is said, lay in thinking we could understand and control the world without organizing cooperatively to do so. In short, fate is created by capitalism and can be surmounted by socialism. Collective action will justify the self-confidence of earlier generations and open the gates to a future human in moral quality as well as in origins and nature.

Since the Soviet Revolution in 1917 this argument has been repeatedly tested. With the substantial qualification that history is not a laboratory, it has been refuted. Neither democratic nor authoritarian socialism has brought into being a society recognized in any consensus of disinterested observers as human in form, scale, and spirit. No form of collectivism so far devised withstands fate. Not that capitalism has been vindicated. Profoundly dynamic, yet refusing deliberately to reckon with consequences, capitalism is clearly a source of fate. But not the only source: human beings are as inhuman collectively as they are individually, and inhumanity arises from purposeful common design as well as from reckless individual enterprise.

FATE AND PRIDE

An irony is not simply an incongruous juxtaposition of circumstances. In the words of a contemporary thinker, an irony consists "of apparently fortuitous incongruities in life which are discovered, upon closer examination, to be not merely fortuitous."[1] Incongruities in history are ironic, then, when there is a hidden link between them. What is the link between the human source and the inhuman quality of our situation today?

It is, I suggest, our exaggerated conception of our own power and goodness. This affects our understanding of the world around. Failing to perceive our own limitations, we fail also to perceive the mystery and independence of the realities we seek to control. The traditional name of this misconception of self and other is "pride." What makes pride a source of fate is that it necessarily leads, in its blindness, to actions that entail unforeseen consequences. These are experienced as fate. The greater our pride and the more ambitious our programs of action, the more massive the fate from which we are likely to suffer.

Although human beings are naturally inclined to be proud, the illusion that we can understand all reality and arrange it as we choose has been greatly encouraged by science and industry. So spectacular have been our technological successes that we have come to see ourselves as masters, potentially if not actually, of all of nature and history. This self-confidence was affirmed in the doctrine of progress and, a handful of dissident thinkers aside, for a century or two was virtually universal. During this time the fate we are now experiencing was blindly created.

It would be well, before proceeding, to examine more closely the blindness in which so many of our troubles began. What have the industrialists, the revolutionaries, and other proud creators of our world failed to see?

The immanence of human beings

We can only tread the surface of reality. We must explore the universe one step at a time and can never see it entire. Pride means neglecting our finitude and the impediment this places on action: our limited ability to calculate the consequences of the things we do and fail to do. Acting with unjustified self-assurance, we encounter the unanticipated results of our deeds in the form of fate. For example, we have

created foul and disorderly cities, but we look on our cities
as we might on scenes of devastation produced by an earth-
quake or hurricane—fearfully but innocently.

The perversity of human beings

Proudly, we do not notice, or we somehow explain away,
the selfishness, callousness, and cruelty that abound wherever
human beings congregate. We banish "sin" from the vocabu-
lary of literate discourse. Then, oblivious of our perversity,
we trust in our power. In this way we become vulnerable
not merely to miscalculation but to malice. Such proud
innocence can be so undiluted that its results are viewed as
purely accidental. The Bolsheviks of 1917, naively assuming
that human evil was a passing historical phenomenon, took
little care to provide against it in the political order they
created. As a result, not merely did they fall short of their
goals; they produced a particularly monstrous regime. But
how was Stalin's government regarded by those who had
laid the groundwork for it and then became its victims? Not
as something they had in their blindness willed, but merely
as a fateful mischance. Another example of moral amnesia,
however, is nearer at hand. How could Americans year after
year have devoted official energies and national resources to
warring on a tiny peasant nation almost wholly unconnected
with American interests? In part because of our innocent
hearts. We were not on guard against the murderous potentialities inherent in Americans as in all human beings. The
war in Vietnam has always seemed to Americans more like a
malicious trick played by history than like a national crime.

The mystery and plenitude of being

Only objects are fully comprehensible and controllable,
and pride therefore objectifies. It strives to understand the
spiritual as physical, the individual as general, the spontaneous as necessary. Pride is intolerant of all that cannot be
rationally explained and deliberately organized. It was not
because the French bourgeoisie were philistines that they
were outraged by painters such as Cézanne and Renoir but

because they sensed that such painters were bringing to light aspects of reality that did not lend themselves to rational comprehension and control.

The ultimate interests of the human race

We have been blind not only to the things that are—ourselves and the realities we must deal with—but to the things that ought to be. We have increased our vulnerability to fate by losing sight of what is threatened by the assaults of fate. In America, for example, if any single goal has guided us it is freedom, and our aimlessness is reflected in the emptiness of our concept of freedom. In theory, freedom has come to mean little more than doing and saying what we please. In practice, it has been reduced for many to picking among the trivial alternatives offered in the capitalist marketplace. Pride has stifled our awareness of destiny. This is one reason it has brought us under the sway of fate.

In summary, confidently oblivious of our own finitude and perversity, of the mystery and plenitude of being, and of the true ends of humanity, we unintentionally create and empower fate. Such a state of mind is pride, and pride is thus the hidden link between the two ironically contrasting characteristics of fate—that it is something that befalls us but that we ourselves have created.

Pride is a striving toward ascendancy, a state in which security, prestige, and the gratification of every wish are assured. It is perhaps the strongest of all human inclinations. Frequently, however, it is restrained or concealed. We could not inhabit the earth together unless the will to ascendancy were in various ways curbed by the demands of common life. Pride may live underground, as it were, concealed by social courtesies and nourished by small and inconspicuous victories. Or it may become collective, as in bellicose patriotism, and may then be paradoxically manifest in acts of personal self-sacrifice.

Further, pride at times gives way altogether. When this happens it is replaced, if not by authentic humility, by inclinations that are not toward the expansion of the self but toward its diminution. These are inclinations toward giving up not merely ascendancy but all responsibility. The motive is physical and spiritual security—guaranteed by someone else. The people governed by Dostoevsky's Grand Inquisitor (an exemplar of pride) sought "bread, miracles, and authority." They sought a world without risks, solitude, or doubt, which necessitated the idolatry implicit in absolute obedience. The underlying moral state, replacing pride, may be called "self-abandonment."

Self-abandonment occurs on account of despair. Self-confidence is lost and one seeks to be relieved of selfhood itself. Despair assumes many forms. Enacted in sensuality, dissipation, and suicide, it is present in the obsessive busyness in which there is no thought, happiness, or hope.

Developments of this kind do not lessen the power of fate. The various forms of restraint and concealment leave pride intact, still a source of unanticipated and unwelcome history. Where despair takes hold, the result is only that the self-abandonment of some makes room for the pride of others. People flee into the arms of fate. Some mistake fate for a stable, comprehensible, and agreeable world, while others see it as it is but welcome the destruction it promises. In 1933 many Germans followed Hitler because the Third Reich held out hope of wealth and pleasure, or of savings and employment, fortified against the depredations of some feared group, such as Jews or Communists. In 1945 many remained loyal to Hitler in the face of national defeat and that must have been in many cases because he showed the way to a fiery and mindless death.

Here again, however, we must be wary of elitist over-simplifications. Probably power, wealth, and social standing both attract and encourage pride. Probably common status—political subordination, economic constraint, and social obscurity—are accepted by most of those enduring them by virtue of some mild and pacifying form of despair. But pride and self-abandonment are not proportionate to political, economic, or social standing. Dostoevsky's parable is not only political but also spiritual. Practically everyone is both a Grand Inquisitor and a docile subject—condescending and proud (even if also compassionate, like the Grand Inquisitor), but also fearful of responsibility, hungry for bread, miracles, and authority.

The hidden link between the humanity and inhumanity of fate, then, is the inclination of each one to be something other than a mere human being: to gain the autonomy and transcendence of a god, or the irresponsibility and immanence of a thing. To be merely human is to live by bread which no social arrangements can absolutely assure; by faith and intellect, with all of the uncertainties inherent in both, and not by miracles which smother doubt; and in a state of freedom and, consequently, of anxious responsibility. It is not surprising that we recoil from circumstances as uncomfortable as these. In doing so, however, we give rise to the insubordinate events and powers that constitute fate.

THE ROOTS OF PRIDE

Our subjection to fate has this strange characteristic, that we are guilty for committing the prideful acts that empower fate and yet can be said to commit those acts necessarily. Kant has fully delineated this paradox in his critical philosophy. Common sense denies the paradox and asserts that in some cases our behavior is conditioned and in some cases free. It is doubtful, however, that common sense can couch this view in a coherent ontology, an ontology blending freedom and causal necessity. More tenable is the explicit rejection of ontology, as in Kant, coupled with the principle that we must regard ourselves in two different ways: from the standpoint of moral decision as free and from the standpoint of rational explanation as causally determined.

This would be a far weaker hypothesis than it is were it not confirmed by common experience. One feels helplessly drawn toward acts which one feels guilty for committing. One feels, as age-old religious testimony has it, "in the grip of sin." This experience is present today in the duality which characterizes our consciousness of our historical situation: as unsought and inescapable, yet inexplicably a burden on our conscience. Trying to bear their global responsibilities, Americans often feel at once unfortunate and culpable.

To think for a moment of causal necessity, two principal conditions give rise to pride. One is our physical vulnerability. Our natural situation is unsafe. In order to gain food, clothing, and shelter, and to protect ourselves against others, we must assert a measure of command both over physical reality and over other humans. This command, moreover, must be solidified in hierarchical social and political forms. Seemingly this might be done merely as a matter of humble acquiescence to physical necessity. Under the goading of fear, it is done in a spirit of more or less unrealistic self-exaltation.

The other condition giving rise to pride is our spiritual vulnerability. When every physical danger has been met we become conscious of dangers rooted in our finitude and freedom. In conditions of utmost physical security, we still must grow old and sometime die. We do not know what this will mean to us. Nor, looking back, do we know how or why we have come to be. Hence we feel not only physically, but also metaphysically, unsafe. We fear, beyond ineffectiveness, guilt and condemnation, and beyond loss of life, loss of soul. It may seem that all of this might be humbly borne. Impelled by anxiety, however, we deny that there is a judge over us or that anything in our past acts or present character need make us fearful of judgment. We insist on our ontological sovereignty and our moral innocence.

In view of these conditions human beings can be pitied even in their crimes. Their natural situation is both constraining and tormenting. They have much, in the dispassionate light of reason, to fear; and they naturally experience a concern for eternity to which reason cannot definitively respond. From this point of view, human sin is no more than a natural product of physical and spiritual vulnerability.

To turn now from causal necessity to freedom, however, it must be said that consciousness of the constraints of their natural situation has never enabled human beings to quiet their minds about their laughable and murderous ways of proudly falsifying themselves. In spite of all the deterministic structures of thought they have built and tried to inhabit, they have remained aware of their responsibility for their misdeeds and for their delusory pride. By this inward certainty, which can neither be abandoned nor rationally justified, it is shown us that although we are victims of fate we are not fated to be victims of fate.

The paradox of necessity and freedom may be clarified by noting that pride affirms the very conditions that call it forth. In the pride provoked by our physical and metaphysical vulnerability, we will the very situation in which we experience this vulnerability. It is by imposing, and then suffering, objectification that this happens. In pride we try to reduce realities to knowable and manageable proportions—to objects. To objectify comprehensively is to define the universe as a system of things. These are wholly available for knowledge and use but entirely lacking in mystery and moral significance. Such a universe can be appealing so long as everything seems under control. However, when control is obviously lost, people find that they themselves are mere things, existing in a universe of things. In objectifying reality they have defined themselves in a way which intensifies their consciousness of physical and spiritual vulnerability. ("God is not mocked.") When this happens, pride may be called forth anew or may give way to self-abandonment or humility. Pride and self-abandonment only reinforce the conditions which they falsely make us think we can surmount or escape. They reinforce fate.

While comments such as these may clarify the paradox of causal necessity and moral guilt, they do not resolve it. Our moral situation can be elucidated but not finally and unequivocally explained. To invoke a mystery in this way might seem an unjustified intellectual tactic were it not that the mystery is encountered in everyday moral experience. Pride is universal and irresistible. Anyone attending carefully to inner feelings knows the tireless and subtle nature of pride; even attaining humility calls forth pride. In short, the necessity of pride is not only an intellectual hypothesis but also a matter of clear awareness. Yet each person in his pride accords primacy to himself, and neglects or harms those around him. Consequent feelings of guilt are not assuaged by the most perfect demonstrations of the inevitability of pride.

The realization of simultaneous helplessness and guilt is described with great power by Dostoevsky in *Crime and Punishment*. Raskolnikov was fully responsible for murdering the two women. He could not blame his crime on his poverty or the squalid circumstances in which he lived. Yet he was driven to the crime by a necessity so compelling that it was "as though someone had taken his hand and pulled him along irresistibly, blindly, with supernatural strength."[2]

These are themes embodied in the myth of original sin. Our misdeeds are unavoidable yet inexcusable. In the biblical myth the ultimate origin of the moral situation giving rise to this paradox lies in an unjustified and incomprehensible human revolt against divine governance. In this essay we have recognized something in the nature of an inexplicable primal rebellion in noting that humanity in its pride wills the conditions which it is the essence of pride to try wholly to master.

This is a puzzling and exasperating subject for reflection. My purpose in probing into it as far as I have is not only to trace the roots of fate, but also to reflect on human responsibility. The paradox of necessity and freedom shapes our relations with fate.

It seems that fate is ironic not only in our creating the forces that threaten and enslave us but also in our serving knowingly as their agents. The brute facts of our world maintain their sway not mainly by naked force but by winning compliance even from many who condemn themselves for their compliance.

The experience of being bound to do what one can justly be blamed for doing was pervasive among Americans during the war in Vietnam. Multitudes of Americans felt that the actions their government was carrying out in Vietnam amounted to a crime of immense proportions. Equally widespread, however, was the sensation of being caught in a vast misfortune, a fate of which Americans, no less than the Vietnamese whose homes and lives they were destroying, were the victims. "So bewildered were Americans *by what was happening to them and by what they themselves were doing*," as one writer remarked, "that many came to believe that both in Indo-China and at home the United States had been overtaken by a wholly accidental and therefore wholly absurd fate."[3]

It would of course be too simple to say that all who share a fateful situation, such as American involvement in Vietnam, are equally responsible for it. Responsibility must vary in countless and subtle ways from individual to individual, depending both on attitudes and on actions, and fate must always rest on an indescribably intricate structure of responsibility. Nonetheless, the common notion that in relation to any reprehensible collective deed it is possible to distinguish sharply, or even to know that a sharp distinction exists, between the guilty and the guiltless is unacceptable. It presupposes an unrealistic individualism and optimism. None are so wholly separate from society or so innocent. A society cannot sustain a prolonged and demanding commitment unless it corresponds with strong and enduring attitudes within that society, and an individual can hardly be a member of a society without in some degree and fashion sharing those attitudes. Americans who protested their country's actions in Vietnam may have lessened their guilt for the atrocities that were occurring (and may not have: much self-righteousness was evident among protesters). To think that they thus fully cleared themselves of blame, however, presupposes a simplistic view both of human relationships and of human responsibility.

Fate, then, entails guilt. This is inherent in the irony of fate.

PRIDE, SUFFERING, AND HOPE

The nature and the fateful consequences of pride, as well as the strength of pride in our time, may be clarified by reflecting on contemporary attitudes toward suffering. People today are fiercely intolerant of suffering—not so much in the lives of others (our age does not seem unusually compassionate), but in their own lives. This intolerance reflects several facets of pride. And it brings to our attention another aspect of the irony of fate, that in proudly repudiating suffering, modern man has contributed to the vast amount of suffering undergone in our fated times.

Of course suffering can never be completely acceptable. If it were, it would not be suffering. But it has often been regarded as bearable and potentially fruitful. Such patience has passed. In capitalist advertising and socialist rhetoric alike suffering is denied all legitimacy. The assumption is that life should be enjoyable; so far as it is not, remedial steps should be taken without delay. Capitalists think of these steps in terms of individual acquisition, socialists in terms of institutional reform. From both sides any indifference to a life physically secure and enjoyable is regarded as retrograde. The idea that suffering ought to be patiently, even hopefully, borne (Paul said, "We rejoice in our sufferings"[4]) is incomprehensible to both "conservatives" and "progressives," to both private entrepreneurs and governmental administrators.

How have our views on this matter come to be so uniform and decided? Leaving aside the fact that lessening, or at least promising to lessen, suffering is economically and politically profitable, several reasons are discernible. Each of these tells us something about our pride.

First, not only is our power of avoiding and postponing suffering far greater than ever before; our confidence in that power is greater than ever before. We are less respectful of the inevitable than were past ages. We do not merely strive to lessen suffering, however. One cannot miss in modern rhetoric the alluring thought of a world from which suffering has been altogether banished, a world in which life is reliably enjoyable. We see the continuance of suffering not only as unpleasant but as humiliating; it casts doubt on our understanding and command of the realities around us.

Not only has our power made suffering seem unnecessary; our rationalistic self-assurance has made it seem meaningless. For many in the past, human beings entered through suffering into a mystery in which was hidden the meaning of life. This intuition is evident in the tragedies of the ancient dramatists and of Shakespeare, and it is clearly articulated in Christian doctrine. To acknowledge a mystery, however, requires humility. For most people today, the world around us has only the meanings we assign and impose upon it. Fate contains no mystery and we may pit ourselves against it without compunction.

Finally, not only do we see ourselves as sovereign in power and the universe as a mirror of our own purposes, but we are confident in our moral innocence. For traditional Christianity every person was guilty in the very orientation of his being, an orientation away from God and toward the self and the world. Hence there was no wholly innocent suffering (apart from the suffering of Christ). For many humane and responsible people today, almost all suffering is innocent. Gross misdeeds are committed, but these we are inclined to dismiss as exceptional or to interpret as manifestations of illness rather than moral evil. Our presumed cosmic sovereignty thus causes us few misgivings. Once fully established, it must be beneficent.

It is true, of course, that a great deal of disillusionment has occurred in recent times. Our self-confidence has been shaken. But our basic outlook has not been revised. We are disappointed and perplexed but trustful still of human

power. We look around us, not for meanings which transcend the calculated consequences of our actions, but for
ways in which our command of events can be restored.

Thus throughout our political, economic, and social lives,
the judgment implied constantly and in countless variations
is that human suffering is avoidable, meaningless, and un-
deserved. Twentieth-century Americans have seen innumer-
able examples of the trivial and destructive ends for which
men purposely or accidentally use their industrial power.
Most of us seem still to believe that the happiness of the
human race waits mainly on our discovering and making
prudent arrangements, whether these consist in well-tried institutional forms of the past, in careful measures of reform,
or in radical programs of social and political reconstruction.
The differences among the ideologies are not nearly so great
as we often suppose. In their typical views conservatives,
liberals, and radicals are at one in seeing suffering purely as
an object of conquest and not at all as a source of insight and
wisdom.

With all of our self-confidence, however, we do not have
great hope. What we have instead is assurance—a different
thing. Assurance is the feeling that all is under our control or
at least that it can be. All problems, consequently, are solu-
ble. Hope, on the other hand, is the feeling that all will turn
out well, although not necessarily due to human foresight
and action, and not necessarily in a way empirically manifest
in any individual life or even in all earthly history. For hope,
the good finally reached may be far from the good people
now seek. Summarily, assurance rests on the belief that the
universe is rationally comprehensible, hope on the sense that
the universe is mysteriously in accord with humanity.

Assurance tends to provoke intolerance of suffering because suffering calls into question the grounds of assurance.
Hope moves one to bear suffering in an inquiring and (since
serious inquiry comes about ideally through communication)
communal frame of mind. In the midst of suffering, one
looks for meaning. Suffering brings no automatic benefits.
Rather, it brings temptations to self-pity and resentment and,

hence, can be morally corrosive. The dangers inherent in suffering are intensified by assurance, for suffering necessarily brings a crisis of confidence. Suffering of course threatens hope as well. But hope instills the patient and searching spirit which is indispensable if suffering is to yield wisdom rather than despair.

The absence of hope helps explain why our age is proud and yet strangely close to despair. When our assurance is challenged, nothing remains. Confronting fate, our inner balance is precarious. The suffering brought by fate tempts us to extremes like terrorism and authoritarianism.

Our present hopelessness is apparent in our politics. To avoid despair, we seek assurance. We strive for mastery through supposedly reliable systems, such as capitalism or socialism, or we fall back on authoritative and powerful historical agencies, on parties, nations, or leaders. We search for intellectual security by drawing up programs of action and sketching out ostensible laws of historical development. Modern man relies heavily on such devices. What will happen as they continue, in accordance with the irony of fate, to fail?

The themes of suffering and hope are unfolded in the drama of Doctor Zhivago. Pasternak recounts, in essence, the resistance of one man to the fate set in motion by the Russian Revolution of 1917, a resistance dependent on a willingness to suffer. Zhivago thought in the first stages of the Revolution that the way might be opened for the human possibilities so harshly denied by the Czarist regime. The revolutionaries, however, soon displayed an implacable historical willfulness and, along with this, a complete absence of hope—of openness to the historical future. The Revolution turned into a fate which laid waste the Russian land and people and Zhivago's own life as well—his medical practice, his personal relations, his health. Little survived for Zhivago but a capacity for hope—hope painfully severed from the Revolution and deprived of all reasonable prospects but retained as an indefeasible readiness for experience and life.

In his political detachment, Zhivago was a strange and suspicious figure (like Pasternak himself) in the eyes of the Communists. In his isolation he was vulnerable. But fate did not have the last word even though it disrupted the order of his existence and finally destroyed his life. Immersed in suffering, his own and that of people he loved, he lived without despair his own singular life.

It is tempting, mixing fiction and reality, to contrast Zhivago and Lenin: on one side vulnerability, on the other power; on one side receptivity, on the other will; on one side hope, on the other assurance; finally, on one side a personal life carried on, with all of its suffering, in what Pasternak refers to as "the air of that freedom and unconcern that he [Zhivago] had always emanated,"[5] on the other side, judging from Lenin's last vain and despairing efforts to block the rise of Stalin and the Party bureaucracy, defeat by fate.

People all over the world have found political inspiration in Lenin. Scarcely anyone thinks of Dr. Zhivago as representing a serious political stance. Soviet rulers showed by their hostility to Pasternak, however, that they knew better. They knew that Zhivago embodied an ethos deeply at odds with the political principles they represented, principles which in their magnification of human will were only a manifestation of the political faith of modern man.

2

DESTINY

FATE THREATENS HUMANITY at its center; it threatens the soul. As I suggested in the Prologue, the soul may be understood as the essential self, transcendent and sacred. It may also be understood as destiny.

Destiny is selfhood as a temporal unfoldment. So far as I live a destiny, all that occurs has a place in a life experience that is a gradual disclosure of personal identity. Within the scope of a destiny, nothing merely befalls me, nothing is merely outward and accidental. Every happening plays a part in the actualization of the self.

No one, of course, lives a life manifest as pure destiny. No one can discern in every accident of life the drama of self-actualization. The world surrounding us is often brutally indifferent to the fragile identities that individuals try to establish. In a few individuals, such as religious and patriotic martyrs, even torture and death seem to enter into the substance of an exalted selfhood. But most lives are repeatedly deranged by the assaults of fate.

The concept of destiny implies that selfhood is not merely an abstract and changeless identity transcending the struggle to embody that identity in a concrete life. It is also the struggle itself, for a full human being incorporates the entirety of his past, all that has gone into his making. Hence it must be said, not that one *has* a destiny, but that one *is* a destiny.

29

The limits of reason in the face of destiny are apparent. A person is not something that can be definitively known and simply is what it is, like a tree or a house. A destiny is not a quality, like a color, that belongs to such an object. A person is always more than he or anyone knows about him. He is not only one who is known but also one who knows; and he is one who inquires and discovers. He is a "thought-adventurer," as D. H. Lawrence said. He is also a moral judge and protagonist. He can condemn himself and try to change. To conceive of a *being* who is essentially *becoming* is difficult; defining the terms strictly, it is impossible. But to think of man, that is what must be done.

While destiny is never pure, however, it is real, and it is familiar to all of us. Just as no one has lived a life free altogether of fate, so no one has lived a life lacking all traces of destiny. No one is therefore without intimations of destiny. A person wonders, for example, whether he has chosen the right vocation. This may, to be sure, be thought of merely as a life activity bringing personal pleasure, plentiful remuneration, and the satisfaction of serving others. But something more is suggested by the very term "vocation"— a call, or a summons. To think of my own or another's vocation is to be aware that a human being's life is not to be used in any way that is pleasant or profitable, or even in any way that happens to be helpful to others. It is subject to more ultimate demands. The sense of destiny is particularly poignant in the consciousness of having missed the vocation one ought to have followed. This is a consciousness not merely that one might have been happier or more useful, but that one has not lived the life given to one to live.

Common feelings for friends, mates, and offspring also exemplify our familiarity with destiny. The feeling that a close and enduring marriage does not originate in merely human preferences and choices is apt to be tritely expressed, but it is a compelling intuition. Some relationships cannot be thought of as though they might never have been. One's own children often evoke a sense of destiny. It is easy to feel that the world is a far worse place for them to inhabit than you had anticipated, but it is difficult to regard them merely as products of a biological accident or an imprudent decision.

Good novels may make us conscious of destiny. When they do, it is by brushing away the details that in actual life do not clearly cohere in the form either of fate or destiny and that obscure the significance of our affairs. Not that novels always show us destiny fulfilled. They may show us destiny forsaken: Nicholas Stavrogin, for example, in contrast with Pierre Bezhukov. But they sometimes dissipate the fog of senseless circumstance and hint of meanings that the life of a person has or ought to have. The satisfaction given us, that of feeling that thus it had to be, comes from sensing more strongly than we ordinarily can the necessity inherent in destiny and fate.

To put this in another way, writing a novel, or indeed telling a story in any form, can be a way of searching for meaning. The fateful facts of daily life are sorted out and rearranged in an effort to discover their personal significance. There are also less wise and gentle ways which human beings have of trying to subordinate circumstances to personal unfoldment.

Astrology is one of these. Interest in astrology is apt to be widespread in times of spiritual turmoil and it mirrors an awareness both of fate and of destiny. The former is more obvious: everything from the movement of the stars to the details of daily life is fixed in the patterns of an impersonal universe. But devotees of astrology are not simply fascinated by doom. If the patterns of the universe can be discerned before they have fully had their way, they can be made to serve the ends of personal life. Such an inference is illogical, but spontaneous and nearly inevitable. And it can call forth an image of destiny—of the universe, apparently overwhelming in its infinitude and indifference, actually in subordination to human selfhood.

Do we not sometimes see an effort to convert fate into destiny—an effort that is activist, and directed toward history rather than the physical universe—in political violence? An assassin, for example, is apt to be not only poor and powerless but obsessed with his own insignificance. People of influence and fame represent an alien and menacing world. The act of assassination presents a prospect of shattering these fateful surroundings. For a few days in 1963, a world which occasionally had seemed to be comprised in the destiny of John F. Kennedy appeared suddenly to have been violently rearranged according to the destiny of Lee Harvey Oswald.

That destiny is authentic selfhood helps explain why the connotations of necessity and freedom are both paradoxically present in the concept of destiny. The connotation of necessity is so pronounced that destiny is often confused with fate, and the words are used interchangeably. But if the necessity inherent in destiny were of the same kind as that inherent in fate—external and coercive—destiny would be indistinguishable from fate. In matters of destiny, necessity is personal. What is destined is what must be if you are to be yourself. "Here I stand, I can do no other." Luther's apocryphal words indicate dramatically the personal character of the necessity inherent in destiny. Considering merely what outward circumstances allow, neither Luther nor anyone else has ever been confined to a single choice. But considering who one is and must be, every alternative may melt away.

What is at stake is not a personality structure that one might vacate as though it were a house. Selfhood is not some kind of convenience or device. It is not a means but an end. Nor is it an end of the kind one might set aside in favor of other ends. It is the only end that matters (assuming that selfhood is communal, so that the authentic being of one is not gained at the expense of another). "For what is a man profited, if he gain the whole world and lose his own soul?"

Living one's destiny, then, is an unconditional moral imperative. Nevertheless, it cannot be done by adhering to moral rules. Each one must live one's own particular and incomparable life. Moral rules give only general guidance. One who in every thought and act perfectly satisfied the moral code but did no more than that would be a phantom of rectitude, lacking the mystery and plenitude of humanity. But generality is not the only limitation inherent in the moral law. Imperfect applicability is another. Rarely can all relevant rules be followed in any concrete situation. This means that ordinarily one rule cannot be obeyed without violating another. But finally, in reflecting on the relationship of destiny and morality, it is necessary to acknowledge the limitations not only of moral law but also of human nature. Even if the moral law were fully concrete and perfectly applicable, the perfection to be achieved by obeying it in every detail would be beyond anyone. In all lives there are serious moral failures; we fail to recognize this because many such failures are unspectacular and hence are not noticed widely, and perhaps are not noticed even by those committing them. A destiny may be accomplished, however, in spite of such failures. This is the theme of the Christian doctrine of forgiveness and an insight not wholly strange to the Hellenic mind, as is shown by the Oedipus drama. The moral law bespeaks our subjection to an absolute claim. This, however, is a claim that transcends every rule and becomes concrete only as a destiny.

Nor is destiny found through applying scientific, as distinguished from moral, principles. A theory of human nature can be nothing better than one possible interpretation of experience, incomplete and disputable. And it necessarily leaves normative issues undecided. The potential usefulness of certain theories of motivation, like those of Marx or Freud, is beyond reasonable doubt. The best uses for such theories, however, become apparent only in the context of a destiny. The self in its encompassing and indefinable fullness is not something we can dispassionately investigate and manage. It is not only an object but also an irreducible subject, the ground upon which psychological and sociological investigations are undertaken and the ultimate ends of self-management and social reform decided.

Destiny is freedom, and its intrinsic necessity is the inviolable demand of freedom upon us. But freedom is not caprice. It is, to be sure, living one's own life rather than the life prescribed by another. But that means living under the

authority of one's own genuine being and not at the dictate of impulses or prospective pleasures. Hence destiny entails living at once freely and as one must.

The concept of destiny pertains to persons, not to objects
in space and time. Accordingly, it cannot be pointed to or
precisely described, as can a natural phenomenon. It must be
spoken of evocatively, equivocally, symbolically. It is not
merely hard to discover one's destiny; it is possible to doubt
or forget its very existence.

Hints of destiny are contained in almost everything of
value. The moral law, for example, seems to tell me that the
person I actually am is not the same as the person I ought to
be and that I must concentrate upon reaching that unrealized,
beckoning identity. In this way every moral imperative is an
intimation of destiny. Truth also serves as such an intimation.
It does this through the absolute respect it inspires. How
could such respect be appropriate unless ultimate being
were congruous with the striving of the self toward its own
genuine reality—which is implied by the concept of destiny?
Beauty, finally, provides sensuous suggestions of this con-
gruity. Many great paintings, for example, show us a world
that seems perfectly shaped and proportioned to the demands
of the essential self, and many musical works can be heard
as representations of destiny. These are only hints, however,
not evidence of the sort we look for in investigating the objective world.

The concept of life is often invoked in an effort to charac-
terize human existence as it ought to be. But destiny is not
life, at least not life alone. We recognize this in our contempt for anyone who would sacrifice everything merely to
survive. We recognize it also in our respect for martyrs.
Here we seem to sense that a person can lose life itself yet
somehow gain substantial being.

Destiny is paradoxical. It may take the form of righteousness achieved in spite of guilt (affirmed by Paul as a possibility inherent in the mercy of God), truth found in ignorance (suggested by Socrates' serene professions of ignorance
in the face of death), beauty apparent in ugliness (as in the

face of Abraham Lincoln), dignity inseparable from horror and suffering (encountered in heroes of tragic drama such as Oedipus). In the presence of a destiny we feel that all is as it should be even though we have difficulty in explaining in what way or why this is so.

Destiny does not belong exclusively to great figures, however. We have some inkling that it belongs to every human being without exception. We say that each one possesses "infinite value" and is "an end and not merely a means." We speak of "the dignity of the individual." What do we mean? Not that every person in his present, manifest existence compels respect, for that is not so. Nor do we mean that every person compels respect by virtue of his potentialities; we defend the dignity of those who are mentally retarded and hopelessly ill. We cannot be referring to any objective reality or natural potentiality, to anything that can be pointed to or precisely described. This is not simply because we are spiritually unsettled and philosophically confused. Even the greatest writers have had to speak of some things indirectly, as is done through myths. But the concept of destiny does provide us with a word and an idea. It suggests how we can say and think crudely what we obscurely feel: that a human being—every human being—is meant for a majesty that demands acknowledgement even where it is indiscernible or irrevocably lost.

THE UNIVERSALITY OF DESTINY

Although a destiny is thoroughly personal—my destiny, or yours—we should not infer that it is mine and in no way yours, or yours and in no way mine, as though destiny were divisive. A destiny is antithetical to fate but not to another destiny. A destiny is simultaneously personal and communal. It is not possible to describe unambiguously the relationship of destinies, but experience shows forth unmistakably the general character of this relationship.

Serious communication and genuine love do not bring a loss of personal being but rather enhancement. I find my own being through my links with others. When defiiance is necessary, it is not for the sake of exclusive selfhood but for the sake of genuine connections. We set ourselves against society and the state because they keep us from freely expressing ourselves to one another. We resist conformity and coercion because we desire to be freely related, not because we wish to be separate and alone. We know that personal being is not found in the latter state.

That I am fully myself only so far as I am fully united with others—that personal being and community are not in mutual tension—is difficult to understand because of the process of objectification which it is in the nature of reason to carry out. Love and communication are not relationships among objects. Hence objectification clouds the truth that persons can be absolutely distinct, each one a particular self and no other, yet united. The analogy of society and organism is sometimes employed in an effort to make this comprehensible, but to little avail. Members of a genuine community are not simply functional parts of an organized totality, and the functional parts of organisms do not address, listen to, and love one another.

Yet experience seems to testify clearly to what reason is unable to explain. I find that my own being is established and enlarged by entering into communal relations with others and in that way alone. The mutual presence of human beings creates the only environment in which personal being is able to achieve existence and flourish. This, I suggest, is the key to understanding the relationship of destinies.

I find my own destiny in discerning and consenting to yours. To communicate seriously is to inquire into destinies. To love is to envision a destiny for the one who is loved and to help that destiny become a reality. Merely to think of all destinies as harmonious and mutually supportive, however, would not quite suffice. It would, indeed, objectify personal relationships. Experience suggests that all destinies are a single destiny.

Looking beyond intimate relationships, out over the world and back into the past, we find that every destiny commands attention. Those whom we call "great" are worthy of study not so much because they are examples (sometimes they do not serve us in that way at all) and not because they alone have destinies, but because they clearly show forth destiny and each one of us is in some sense a participant in every destiny. Nor do great rulers and writers demand our notice merely because of their influence on our own times and circumstances. If we were suddenly to come upon records of an outstanding figure hitherto completely unknown, and altogether without influence on our own society and times, we would still feel ourselves in the presence of something demanding our attention. The truth is that encountering a destiny we feel ourselves in the presence of a reality that is comprehensively human, a reality involving all of us and forbidding indifference.

Further, not only do I experience other destinies as my own, but I experience my own destiny as an act of participation in the destiny of humanity as well. This is at least one of the truths implicit in the Christian doctrine of vicarious suffering; the suffering of one person may enter into the destinies of others. I am alienated only from those who bow down to fate. In becoming alive to my destiny I find myself, however deeply in conflict with established society I may be, mysteriously taking part in the central affairs of the human race. In trying to resist the reigning forms of fate and live a destiny, I may be forced into solitude. But the solitude required by a destiny must be informed with an attentiveness and availability which renders it a relationship with all humankind.

It is a sign of the universality of destiny that living a destiny is a cultural venture. It would be impossible without the art, philosophy, and religion inherited from the past. Drawing on this inheritance is not so logical a procedure as merely applying general standards to my own particular case. A culture does not yield a code of clear standards, and the particularity of a destiny gives every serious life a primordial character. But we would be unprepared to live a destiny without the insights that are given us by artists, thinkers, and religious leaders. We do not attend to masterpieces of art and thought, or to scriptures, mainly to draw usable lessons from them but to participate in the common humanity which they express and which, in my own destiny, I must enact.

Fate is collective, destiny communal. Living a fate often is responding without thought to the requirements and enticements of established society. Hence, although fate may be suffered in a state of excruciating loneliness, we can in contemplating fate follow the example of Plato, who studied man by scrutinizing the political order. Fate is written in large letters in the public world. Destiny is less visible.

Destiny bars thoughtless conformity with social and governmental expectations. Hence destiny is not so plainly manifest in historical realities and events as is fate. This, however, does not mean that destiny is realized by detached individuals. Destiny is not found within the sphere of the individual as contrasted with that of society but within the sphere of community—as contrasted with that of society. Although society requires conformity, community is entered into through a very different kind of act: communication. I cannot follow the counsel of John Stuart Mill and seek selfhood in a private sphere of "self-regarding" acts. I have to search out other destinies as well as my own, and it is this in which all serious communication—in art, philosophy, and religion, in friendship, teaching, and politics—is engaged.

THE IRONY OF DESTINY

To speak of choosing your own destiny, as we so often do, reflects a misunderstanding of human beings and their powers—a misunderstanding at the heart of the present crisis of civilization. Perhaps people can create styles of life and control the general order of their daily existence. But their destinies must be given them.

This is indicated by the word "destiny" itself, with its connotation of necessity. One carries out a destiny under constraint and not as an act of play, improvisation, or spontaneous self-expression. The constraint comes from the life one feels called upon to live. That destiny is required of one, rather than freely chosen, is evident when fidelity to a destiny requires risking one's life. This happens frequently, as with young people in a nation at war or citizens confronting a tyrant, and when it does selfhood may become a sovereign which can command any sacrifice. People do not ordinarily invent so inexorable a master.

The givenness of destiny is also disclosed in the ways we think of personal identity. Even in this self-assertive age people speak of discovering, not creating, themselves. They are concerned with a selfhood that is not yet fully real and yet in some sense is established and ordained, since the task is to find it. This paradox, which defines the structure of destiny, is concisely stated in the maxim that you must become who you are.

I would not like utterly to sever the concepts of destiny and freedom, however. Hence it is well to note that even if destiny is defined as freedom, it still comes to us as something given and required. Freedom is not fully realized in arbitrary choice but only in the act of creation, in bringing forth some reality (perhaps a work of art or perhaps simply one's own performance of an ordinary daily task) which asserts its own singular being apart from every other such reality and in doing so defines and discloses the distinctive being of the creator. In that act one is exalted by the consciousness of stepping forth from dark scenes of struggle and uncertainty into light and reality. To be free is to be yourself; to be yourself fully and accurately, however, is to be creative. Freedom and creativity in the last analysis are identical. Creativity, however, is an object of hope and not of will. It depends on insight ("inspiration") of a kind that cannot be deliberately called forth. Thinking of the greatest creative figures, and of their having lived as though under the orders of a transcendental authority, we realize that freedom is given, as destiny is given, and contains nothing that is willed or capricious.

Awakening to my destiny is in some ways like encountering another person. It is meeting someone who comes from beyond the sphere of my own will and choice. Even my responsibility for my destiny is not wholly unlike my responsibility for another person—to be open and supportive. Realizing a destiny is creative but not willful. Just as artistic creativity originates, according to common accounts, in the discovery that one is given a vision that must be expressed, so bringing a destiny to reality begins in the discovery that one is given a selfhood that must be lived.

Matching the irony of fate, then, is the irony of destiny. Fate comes upon us from without and it comes destructively, as a violent or seductive enemy of personal being. Yet fate is willed by the one who suffers it. Destiny is selfhood, the temporal unfoldment and realization of authentic identity. Yet destiny is given and cannot be willed.

By what or whom is destiny given? Not by nature, however we conceive of nature: if as a system of universals, the singularity of destiny would be inexplicable; if as a causal order, the necessity inherent in destiny would be indistinguishable from that of fate; if as vital force, destiny would be reduced to life. Destiny does not consist in the fulfillment of potentialities, for the potentialities of a human being are not, as we imagine, a complete and harmonious version of that human being latent in nature. They are indeterminate (we read back into someone the potentialities for doing what has already been done), far too manifold and discordant all to be realized, and, many of them, destructive. Destiny shows what human nature can be and ought to be, but it is destiny, and not prior rational insight, that shows this. In this sense, a destiny is a disclosure of natural law. But one must beware of certain views that the concept of natural law suggests: that human behavior is lawfully recurrent and rationally knowable and that thereby moral laws can be rationally prescribed. Destiny reveals humanity as genuinely temporal and this means, as Henri Bergson brought out so eloquently, discordant both in fact and norm with all prior rational determinations.

Nor is destiny given by society. If it were, real conflict between the individual (that is, destiny) and society would be impossible. It can be argued that this indeed is the case, that every apparent conflict between individual and society is really social—a conflict within society. Thus, Socrates was only acting out the disintegration of Hellenic culture, Jesus the humanization and universalization of Judaism. Such an argument would not be wholly wrong. But it would abstract from the same reality that is left out of account if destiny is interpreted as a product of nature: the single, irreducible, and distinct personality. Explaining the person in terms of society requires one to look at reality as though it were altogether a set of objects available for detached observation even though immediate personal exprience, including mysteries which we call by such names as "subjectivity" and "concreteness," informs us conclusively that it is not. One who remains at the center of his personal being knows that seeing the individual as a function of social forms and forces depends on a deliberate, although perhaps in some ways useful, narrowing of vision. Seen more comprehensively, society is an aspect of the individual.

Destiny is given by something beyond nature and society, something that may be referred to as "transcendence." This is a term with religious overtones, and I would not want these to be overlooked or neglected. We have our origin as destined beings—destined, rather than merely natural or social—in transcendence. Attitudes partaking of awe and trust are inseparable from the realization of this condition.

Destiny, however, need not be given any particular creedal definition. As a Christian, I believe that the relationship between humanity and transcendence is fully and truly disclosed in Christ. At the same time, I do not believe that Christians alone have access to transcendence. All in diverse ways may touch the hem of Christ's garment. Christ as Logos is present in all beautiful art, true thought, and righteous activity. Destiny is a call on every person and can be interpreted and lived in the terms of a variety of religious creeds.

Destiny can also be discerned and lived outside of all religious creeds. "Transcendence" is a word with agnostic (but not atheistic) overtones. One may refer to transcendence as a way of barring ascriptions of immanence. Used in this way, the term enables us to acknowledge the mystery of our origins without involving ourselves in doctrinal or ecclesiastical commitments. And it performs a highly useful negative function: it warns against tracing our being back to any finite source, reducing ourselves in this way to the dimensions of a particular human category. Thus, thinking of the source of our being as transcendent inhibits us from exaggerating the wisdom, power, and virtue of any human agency. If destiny were attributed to any immanent being the result would inevitably be idolatry—of an intellectual guide, a party leader, or a set of technical experts. That this is not merely conjectural is shown by the worshipful regard in which certain intellectual leaders such as Marx and political heroes such as Lenin are widely held. One who lived his destiny agnostically would not lack a consciousness of something sacred undergirding and illuminating existence. This consciousness would be inherent in his sense of the authority and universality of destiny. It would not, however, be expressed in any creedal or liturgical forms.

In restraining the human impulse to worship human agencies, the concept of transcendence guards the sense of unconditionality that is present in the consciousness of destiny. In striving to uncover my own identity I am not interested merely in who or what I *happen* to be—in a self that is no more than a product of circumstances. Such a self would be accidental. I seek acquaintance with my essential being, the content of the inviolable necessity that belongs to destiny. I must therefore look beyond all circumstances, whether natural or social. The concept of transcendence reminds us of this. It stands in the way of the crime human beings have committed in countless forms throughout his-

tory—the crime inherent in all crime—that of reducing the
essential human being to an accidental manifestation: to the
slave, the barbarian, the heretic, the worker, the capitalist, the
Jew, the black.

At this point, destiny can be defined both more fully and
more succinctly than hitherto. It is essential selfhood, enacted in time, and given by transcendence. Personal being is
essentially bipolar, temporal in reality and transcendental in
origin. For many people today, however, transcendence is
apt to be a troublesome concept. Does it refer to anything
real, to anything with which a relationship is possible?

TRANSCENDENCE AND RECEPTIVITY

In the age of exploration, science, industry, and revolution,
the age that has brought us to our present fateful impasse,
the human stance has been more often one of command than
of receptivity. People have aspired to ascendancy, whether
through intellectual progress, economic enterprise, political
action, or a combination of these. They have looked on the
natural and human realities about them as materials lying at
hand, available for investigation and use. They have looked
on their own lives, correspondingly, as comprehensible and
controllable and, hence, at their own disposal. In a word,
transcendence has been denied.

Although numerous disappointments have been suffered,
these attitudes continue to reign in our minds, prompting reliance on human will and inducing an insensitivity to destiny. Many are discouraged, but not to the extent of radi-
cally questioning the entire modern project, that of subordinating all reality to human purpose. Even self-styled conservatives go no further than arguing that we must be more
cautious if we are effectively to command events. Humility is
understood as nothing more than circumspection. The idea
of an altered relationship with being has not entered the
imagination of any major ideological group.

I suggest that the central practical issue of modern life is whether in our struggle to extricate ourselves from fate we only intensify our drive toward universal mastery. I suggest that the central intellectual issue is whether we persist in regarding reality as entirely objective, as made up of things we can know and hence control.

The truth represented by the concept of transcendence is that we can gain no objective, demonstrable knowledge of the overall nature and structure of being. Our concepts have the function of enabling us to grasp realities of a particular kind, realities that are spatial, temporal, and perceptible. These realities are always found, so to speak, inside of being; there is always more beyond them. We delude ourselves when we suppose that our concepts can be extended in order to give us a grasp of the totality of things. We delude ourselves in two ways: concerning our own nature and situation, forgetting that we are within the world and are incapable of attaining a position from which being as a whole can be surveyed, and concerning the nature of being, thinking of it as though it were a gigantic object or assemblage of objects, whereas, as Kant shows, thinking of it in this way leads inevitably into contradictions.

Transcendence is the margin of mystery beyond everything we do know and can know. Considered in relation to transcendence all conceptual knowledge is seen to be not only incomplete but of indeterminate significance. Since we do not know all, we cannot determine exactly what or how much we do know. This affects our knowledge both of being as a whole and of individual realities. Transcendence is discernible on the horizon, as it were, of the world that lies about us. It is also discernible in relation to every entity within the world. In Kantian terms, underlying every thing that we can know is a "thing-in-itself" that we cannot know.

In short, ontological ignorance is inherent in human nature and the human situation. In resisting fate, it is indispensable that this be acknowledged. Doing this is not an act of resignation to darkness and impotence but is rather a refusal to claim an illusory knowledge or command of the sources of destiny. It is meeting the prerequisites of receptivity toward transcendence. Without such receptivity one is unavailable for his destiny. The claim to understand being in itself, lacking objective justification, is an assertion of will and lays the basis for an assertion of historical command which can only empower fate. Whatever Marx's materialism may mean, it is an unwarranted profession of ontological knowledge, and it bears a connection with the proud and fateful character of Marxist regimes.

This has implications also, however, for believers. Receptivity toward transcendence means refusing to try to prove anything concerning God, even his existence. Hence it means declining either to offer any definitive solution to the problem of theodicy (which would be to presume to understand fully and to justify God's ways) or to declare the problem void (which would be implicitly to claim the knowledge that God does not exist). We are in no position to decide such matters. It is apparent that the religious dogmatist and the atheist are akin. Both try to bring everything within the scope of rational explanation. And in spite of conclusions diametrically opposed, both close themselves off from transcendence.

Christianity is a test of receptivity toward transcendence for Christians and non-Christians alike. Christians are bound to say, with Paul, that they have their "treasure in earthen vessels." God and Christ are not contained within any organization or doctrine. Non-Christians as well are called upon to exercise a difficult humility. They cannot foreclose the possibility that Jesus was in truth the Christ.

Receptivity would be vain if nothing ever were received. Receptivity is fulfilled in faith, in a meeting of man and transcendence. But faith is not foreclosure. The worldly organization and cultivation of faith in common with others renders certain creedal definitions and organizational rules inevitable. These entail a measure of hierarchy and exclusiveness. These are not inherent in faith itself, however, but in worldly associations. Faith, like love, is a liberating relationship. In itself, it confirms receptivity.

A person unreservedly receptive toward transcendence would regard his life gratefully rather than possessively. Confronting death—one of the ways transcendence forces itself on us—a person would be as uncertain yet hopeful as Socrates was before drinking the hemlock. In trying by all means to live, we equate destiny with biological life and thus elevate death into an absolutely final fate. We demonstrate the truth of Jesus' dictum that whoever tries to save his life will lose it.

Receptivity toward transcendence is a way of living in time. Because we must die, we never have time enough and thus, trying to "save our lives," we try to rise above time, to organize and fill it, and in this way subordinate it to will. But a deliberately organized temporal totality is never a destiny. The question is whether one can live within time, receiving each moment as a possible disclosure of destiny. If so, one practices dying, for to live within time is to experience deprivations that are irremediable, since one must die and the time at one's disposal is therefore limited. To practice dying, however, is to habituate oneself to looking toward transcendence. Doing this, one discerns in the limits of temporal existence the configurations of destiny and thus finds substance in the ephemeral moment. Lucid finitude becomes a form of participation in transcendence.

To live lucidly in time is to adhere to a virtue that is undramatic but embodies one of the main requirements of humane and hopeful politics—patience. To live without idols, without a rationally comprehensible god or even rational assurance that the universe is godless, and without more than a tentative and partial command of one's own life, necessitates reconciling oneself to time in all of its tedium and suspense. One can do that only through a sense of destiny in which time is seen as an unfoldment rather than erosion of personal being, and death as an encounter with the source of destiny rather than a final victory of fate. We prove ourselves by patience. Lack of patience has much to do with our present enthrallment to fate. We are not patient either with nature or with history. The ideologies reject historical continuity and try to give time significance by bringing it under the sway of will. They express a rejection of time. That rejection is understandable since time spells uncertainty—by the standards of rational knowledge—of all but inevitable death. But only through a conscious and receptive temporality do we make ourselves available to destiny, and this is no less true politically than personally. Political humanity begins in historical patience.

Receptivity is not all of one kind, however. Understanding this is important if one is to perceive the undogmatic and communal implications inherent in the idea of destiny.

FORMS OF RECEPTIVITY

Receptivity can be humanistic or religious, although neither humanism nor religion is necessarily receptive. Humanistic receptivity is a readiness for destiny that relies on no doctrines concerning transcendence and on no forms of worship. It is availability for the life one is called upon to live but claims no knowledge of the source of that life. It is thus agnostic, although reverent and open. Given a clear understanding that the difference between the two kinds of receptivity is one of degree, it can be said that humanistic receptivity has not congealed as faith and is consequently a relatively anthropocentric orientation.

The supreme exemplar of humanistic receptivity is Socrates, moving toward death without terror or anguish, yet ignorant (according to his own professions) of ultimate realities, and indefeasibly rational and inquiring. Socrates' receptivity is manifest in his unremitting availability, evident in the conduct of his philosophic and civic life alike, to the claims upon him of the ultimate good. It is manifest also in the dialogical relationships that he sustained with human beings even at the cost of his life.

A systematic philosophy that is particularly congenial to humanistic receptivity was worked out, over two thousand years later, by Immanuel Kant. According to Kant, we cannot demonstrably know either that God does or does not exist, hence both religious dogmatism and atheism are out of place. Presupposing a strict definition of knowledge, we are bound to be agnostic. Nonetheless, ultimate being is not beyond all insight and surmise. It enters human awareness in various ways—in the consciousness of duty and in the experience of sublimity, for example. Although ultimate being cannot be scientifically known, it governs our lives by drawing us toward truth and holiness. Humans should be uncompromisingly rational, holding free of all dogma, religious and atheistic alike. They should at the same time live in a hopeful and exploratory relationship with ultimate being, or transcendence.

Possibilities for a noble, if arduous, form of humanistic receptivity are suggested by tragic drama. The tragic vision offers no explicit concept of transcendence and thus no encouragement to the otherworldliness characteristic of some kinds of traditional religious piety. At the same time, it precludes the facile worldliness in which the sphere of ordinary human experience is assumed to be all-inclusive and fully satisfying. The greatest human beings and the most imposing human works are seen in the shadow of doom. Yet spectators of tragic drama do not experience despair but something very different: a strange conviction that all is inexplicably justified, or redeemed. Evoking the mysterious glory that may be present in necessity and suffering, tragic writers such as Sophocles and Shakespeare often provide a poignant consciousness of destiny.

Humanistic receptivity is at once transcendental and skeptical. Religious receptivity entails a more definite commitment and hence presupposes certain concepts of transcendence. Such concepts often come into conflict with receptivity. They do not necessarily do so, however, as suggested by Augustine's dictum that we believe in order to understand. Faith may call forth rational inquiry. Just as believers must acknowledge the possibility of reverent doubt, humanists must acknowledge the possibility of receptive faith.

Christianity in practice has often lacked receptivity, owing primarily to the dogmatism and intolerance into which Christians have been drawn by faith in the uniqueness and finality of the revelation accomplished by the life of Christ. Christianity in its basic import, however, suggests that faith in essence is a kind of unwavering attentiveness in relation to transcendence. The Christian theme is "Christ crucified, unto the Jews a stumblingblock, and unto the Greeks foolishness"—unto "Jews," unto all who wish for a visibly glorious Messiah, a stumblingblock because Jesus did not assume royal governance over the earth but died, scorned by all; unto "Greeks," unto those who refuse any truth not validated by reason, foolishness because the infinite is held to have been incarnate in the finite—a manifest absurdity. To Jews and Greeks alike the Christian response, phrased in countless variations, is that human beings cannot judge the divine. They must divest themselves of preconceptions and listen to God as God has chosen to address them. "Blessed is he, whosoever shall not be offended in me."[1] Reduced to its minimal meaning, this may be interpreted as a call for receptivity, for listening.

Admittedly, this is to construe Christianity according to principles usually associated more with the Old Testament than with the New. According to these principles, God is communal. His relationship to human beings is dialogical, and fidelity to God requires above all else attentiveness. But these principles can readily be applied to Christianity. This is indicated by the Christian doctrine that God is revealed not only in the New Testament but in the Old as well. It is indicated also by the fact that Christians have from the earliest ages of theology regarded Christ as God's Word—as a way in which God addressed humanity.

In the Christian view all that makes up fate—not only alien and destructive historical forces but even death—has come from the efforts of human beings to create their own destiny rather than live the destiny given to them. Mythically described as the sin of Adam, they try to take their lives away from God and into their own possession. As a consequence, deprived of the life given by God, death impends over them as final extinction.

The life of Jesus was pure destiny. Jesus was the Messiah in that through his life every human being is given access to a destiny of his own. Not that Jesus was untouched by fate. In the crucifixion he suffered so fearful a fate that even his followers thought that he had been destroyed. However, for a few, the first Christians, this impression was suddenly and unexpectedly dispelled. The resurrection became a symbol of the faith that through the crucifixion God had established his presence at the heart of fate, thus making it possible for each one to enter into the darkness of fate without being destroyed.

This faith is expressed by construing the life of Jesus as the axis of history. All earthly events lead to and follow from that single sovereign event. This is not mere pious exaggeration, lacking all logic. A life that is pure destiny cannot be within history; history must be within that life. And if that life is God's, and is open to humankind, then it affects every person. It redirects history and transforms the human situation. Henceforth, the life of Jesus is not merely a dramatic memory, like the lives of Julius Caesar, Leonardo da Vinci, and other great figures. It lays out the possibilities and imperatives faced by every human being. Jesus brought a transfigured universe—"new heavens and a new earth."

As an incarnation of the meaning of history, and thus of the overall character of reality, Jesus was the Logos. He established and disclosed the fundamental harmony of being and humanity, of cosmos and personality. In the fires of the crucifixion the universe was recast as a "vale of soul-making"—a setting for the working out of destinies. The resurrection, whatever its empirical basis, was the symbol through which the first Christians testified to their faith that through the life and death of Jesus, fate—even in the form of death—had been subordinated to personal being.

Jesus was the Logos not simply because he embodied the meaning of all things, however. He also was the disclosure of that meaning—the Logos as divine speech. The universe transfigured by the crucifixion and resurrection was made available to the human race but not forced upon them. The Kingdom of Heaven was not to be established by violence.

In view of the communality of the God of Christ, Christianity must be interpreted in terms of freedom. As recast in the life of Jesus, the universe is open to the unrestricted living of destinies. These destinies cannot be easy. Before the resurrection must come the crucifixion. The grain of wheat must fall into the earth and die. This is to say that fate cannot be evaded but is overcome by being suffered. Nonetheless, Christianity offers destiny and consequently freedom. It is perverted when it is turned into a demand for dogmatic belief or rigid morality. The grain of wheat that falls into the earth and dies brings forth much fruit. "Ye shall know the truth and the truth shall make you free."[2] I am here accepting the implications of Dostoevsky's "Legend of the Grand Inquisitor." The faith repudiated by the Grand Inquisitor deprives human beings of sure and plentiful bread which makes physical life secure and agreeable, and of miracles and authority which render spiritual life easy. It is a cruel faith in doing this. It is cruel, however, only in requiring each one to live out of one's own understanding of Christ and destiny—that is, freely. Such, Dostoevsky implies, is true Christianity.

The difference between humanistic and religious receptivity, then, concerns the source of destiny. Socrates' superiority to fate derived from his certainty of something he could not name or describe. Christian martyrs such as Paul of Tarsus and Thomas Becket found in Christ the certainty that enabled them to walk unharmed in the furnace of fate. This difference can be usefully discussed but not definitively resolved. Those on the two sides can clarify their choices through inquiring communication but cannot show by rationally compelling arguments that one position or the other should be adopted by all. It is destiny, so to speak, that decides.

For all who try to live receptively, however, whether on humanistic or religious grounds, there is an ancient intellectual discipline that can help. This is philosophy. As suggested by the literal meaning of the word—love of wisdom—philosophy is better understood as an activity than as an established doctrine. It is the activity of thinking about questions we must answer to live but ordinarily answer unreflectively and even unconsciously. What should we live for? What is truth? Need we concern ourselves with beauty? Philosophy offers doctrines, but it also challenges and destroys doctrines and in this way may clear our minds. It lessens our willingness to accept theories as unconditionally as we often do.

Modern man has a weakness for theories because theories promise a strong and reliable grasp of reality. With theoretical command there can be practical command. Hence the modern world is filled with self-confident disciples of theorists such as Marx and Freud, and modern political life is fervent and disputatious to a degree that ill-suits an age proud of its rationality and often condescending toward the scholasticism of the Middle Ages. If in the past the chief obstacle to receptivity has been religious dogmatism, today it may well be the obsession with finding the true master theory. Genuine philosophical reflection would help greatly to deliver us from this obsession.

Philosophy is persistent questioning. It penetrates, in its persistence, to those issues beyond which no further issues can be found. It does not necessarily lead to skepticism, as the history of philosophy demonstrates. It does not rule out science or faith, and it does not condemn comprehensive theories so long as they can be questioned and changed. Philosophy does not deny the intellectual right of someone to be a Christian, Marxist, or Freudian. But it does call on us to clarify the epistemology of our commitments, to distinguish what we know from what we believe beyond all evidence and reason, and above all to remain within the sphere of personal reflection and common inquiry. It helps to free us from violent certainties and to instill a communal receptivity—a disposition to refrain from trying to force others into doctrinal frameworks but only to accompany them in thinking. Philosophy cannot give us our destinies. No rational activity, and no human activity of any kind, can. But it can make us more accessible to our destinies. It can enhance our openness both toward human beings and toward transcendence, and it can do this whether our persuasion is humanistic or religious. Philosophy can help us remember that intellectual masters such as Marx and Freud are not secular messiahs who provide a final understanding of humanity and its fate, and that neither social reorganization nor psychotherapy will lead to selfhood except under guidance from a sense of destiny which they cannot themselves provide. Also, philosophy can help us realize that scientific knowledge and religious faith differ both in character and object and that confusing them does violence alike to the integrity of science and the majesty of God.

In summary, authentic selfhood is destiny and realizing one's destiny depends on willingness to receive it. Such willingness may be either humanistic or religious, and it is apt to be more sure and lucid if it is also philosophical. But this brings us to an important question. If receptivity is the highest standard of personal conduct, is action condemned? This question relates not only to the meaning of receptivity but also to politics and its place in human destiny, for politics is the master form of action.

ACTION AND DESTINY

Although modern man has tended to interpret all of his relations with reality in terms of action, and has in this way jeopardized his destiny, action cannot be repudiated. To offer so simplistic a response would be to oppose one error with another.

In reflecting on this matter, it is easy to go astray by attending only to the effects that an individual's actions have on the world around him. The modern faith in action has caused these effects often to be ridiculously exaggerated. We are not infrequently given to understand (particularly by civic groups trying to heighten democratic morale) that a single determined individual is likely to have a decisive impact on the affairs of the body politic. In our infatuation with action we may unthinkingly accept such images of personal power. If, however, we divest ourselves of civic-minded illusions (which ordinary voters may be more likely than idealistic intellectuals to do), we realize that only in exceptional instances does a single individual appreciably affect the course of events and that normally even high officials leave only faint historical traces behind them. At this point it is easy to conclude that action is pointless.

Perhaps it is, for the world and history. But action can never be pointless for the one who acts. In the first place, it is necessary to act simply in order consciously and deliberately to be. By acting you commit yourself to particular principles and relationships. You take a position and in this way give yourself marks of identification. By not acting, on the other hand, you hold back from being anyone in particular—or, more accurately, from conscious responsibility for being anyone in particular. This is why inaction is tempting. It seems to be a way of not being finite and fallible. It is, of course, a form of self-deception. To choose not to act is still to choose, and to choose to live carelessly and thoughtlessly is to be finite and fallible. In this sense action is unavoidable. To repudiate action is to cultivate illusions of infinitude and innocence.

In the second place, you must act not only in order consciously to be someone in particular, but you must act also in order to confirm the understanding and faith that is the substance of inner life. St. John speaks of "doing the truth." To accept a principle and then fail to act upon it is in some fashion to revoke the principle. The ideal of contemplation is questionable. It suggests a posture unsuitable to a free and immanent being. Only in action are inner certitudes confirmed as sincere and as appropriate for human minds.

In a word, for one in whose life there is no action, there can be no destiny either. Underlying particularity of being and integrity of belief, action is an indispensable determinant of selfhood. To resist illusions of mastery with an ethos of inaction would leave fate unopposed.

How, then, can we act and at the same time be sure that we do not subvert the true principle of action by forgetting, on one side, our own finitude and fallibility and, on the other side, the mystery and dignity of those on whom we act? It would be possible to suggest rules, such as the one developed by the British philosopher Bernard Bosanquet. According to Bosanquet, the aim of political action should be to "hinder hindrances" to the realization of a good life, not to try directly to create such a life. Another rule designed to recognize, and thus keep one reminded of, one's situation as human and not divine is that of exemplary action. According to this standard one should do that which one is convinced all, or all within a specific category, should do. Thus one may calculate consequences by asking what would happen if all were to act in a certain way, and also recognize that the consequences of one's own particular act may be nil; at the same time, one's action constitutes a statement and is thus an expression of communality. Such rules as these can have considerable value. In these reflections, however, we are trying to survey a large area and must therefore take only those steps that are essential. Accordingly, I shall suggest a standard of action that seems to derive more directly than any other from the concept of destiny.

We may call it simply the standard of necessity. We should try to discover and carry out the action that we are bound to carry out—the action that we cannot fail to carry out without betraying our own being. In Ernest Hemingway's *For Whom the Bell Tolls,* the guerrilla leader, Pilar, tells the worried Robert Jordan on the eve of a highly dangerous military operation, "All will be well, *Inglés*. It is for this that we are born."³ Thus is expressed the sense of an action required by destiny.

Such action would not necessarily be either purely expediential or purely moral. Probable results must be taken into account but cannot be decisive in any morally serious situation. Moral rules also must be taken into account, but a valid decision cannot be merely deduced from a moral rule and it may even violate a moral rule, as did Dietrich Bonhoeffer's decision to engage in a murder conspiracy against Hitler. Reflecting on both practical aims and moral norms, one tries to find the insight that will make it possible to say with the apocryphal Luther, "Here I stand; I can do no other."

Contemporary politics again and again reflects the assumption that good government depends primarily on our deciding what we want and how to obtain it. Political failures are attributed to a lack either of resolution or of skill. Leaders are expected to have armories full of plans and proposals. But such attitudes derive from the notion that we can and should be altogether in control of circumstances. It is that notion itself, casting circumstances as fate, and not indecisiveness or ineptitude, that is the primary source of our troubles. We do not in our politics very often have the historical insight to see, or the historical patience to wait until we can see, the course of action that imposes on us the conviction that we "can do no other."

Perhaps nothing is so indispensable to political leadership as a consciousness of common destiny. Political leaders should come before us with an idea of the lives that they and the rest of us are called upon to live, and they should be capable of making this idea a source of common discussion and finally of decision.

Not that we thus would solve all of our problems. So habitually do we think in terms of solutions that care is needed not to interpret the idea of destiny as a way of attacking our problems. Solutions of any complete and final sort are not available for some of our problems. Destiny is discovered and lived not only by solving problems but also by embodying unsolved problems in the general form of one's life. This is exemplified in the chronic illnesses with which some of the great figures of the past, like Dostoevsky, have had to contend.

A receptive politics is exemplified in the career of at least one statesman, Abraham Lincoln. It is plain in the example of Lincoln that receptivity does not entail inaction; Lincoln possessed uncommon strength and resolution. That he represented a political standard other than effective action, however, is indicated by his suffering—by the fact not just that he suffered but that suffering suffused his whole being and entered into the essence of his leadership. It was as though all the agony of the Civil War was lived through by this one man. His suffering, moreover, was perfectly communicated to the American people, not only by the eloquence of his speeches but by the eloquence of his demeanor. If the question as to how it happened that the ordeal of a whole nation was so powerfully expressed in the ordeal of a single human being has an answer, it may lie in his awareness of a destiny indistinguishably his own and common to all Americans and even to all human beings—a destiny worked out in a great national catastrophe.

It was in the spirit of a presidency marked by suffering and grounded in a poignant consciousness of destiny that Lincoln asserted that he only did the things that he had to do. He disclaimed any control of events but "confessed plainly" that events had controlled him. He disclaimed even having a policy and asserted that he only did "what seemed best as each day came."[4] He was a leader possessed to a singular degree of the prophetic vision that dissipates willfulness while both inspiring and restraining action. By keeping the nation united and bringing an end to slavery, Lincoln had a greater effect on American history than any other president. What guided him, however, was only necessity as he understood it—the necessity intimated in events and the moral law and deriving ultimately, in Lincoln's faith, from the will of God.

Lincoln is known for his compassion. For necessity to be discerned, the human relationships inherent in action must be subordinated to relationships of another kind.

LOVE AND DESTINY

Love is "without fear," according to St. John. Love is without fear because in its fullness it is a discerning of destinies. It is the realization of a peculiar significance in another person—a significance by virtue of which that person is not a mere fact in the world. Love is awareness of an identity that is not visible to detached observation—an identity given from beyond the world and worked out in a free and unforeseeable integration of past and future.

Love is without fear because in discerning destinies it dissolves fate. To be subject to fate is to be surrounded by realities that are alien and threatening. Love discovers that those realities are not wholly what they appear to be. In its supreme moments it does this even when those realities appear to be murderously threatening. The classical symbol of such love is Christ on the cross, manifesting love for all human beings in spite of and even through the crucifixion. By this love not only was the fate of the crucified Christ transformed into a destiny but so was the fate of the crucifiers, for whose forgiveness Christ prayed.

Love is the power of understanding the universe as a threatre for the fulfillment of destinies. By dissipating the fateful configurations created by human beings in their fear and hatred of one another, it perceives possibilities for authentic human life. Under the eyes of love, the universe loses the stark factuality of fate. This is not because fate is dismissed as illusory but because it is seen to be inconclusive.

In not being decided by appearances, love is strange, even incomprehensible. It more or less ignores, and may even deny, what dispassionate observation would tell us about other persons. In this sense love is unreasonable and indiscriminate. It cannot say, and ordinarily refuses even to try to say, why it is bestowed here rather than there. It is merciful, capable of disregarding established guilt. It tends to be universal and egalitarian, challenging the distinctions and hierarchies always present in an established social order.

As strange as it is, love is plainly real, encountered in various forms in daily experience. Even romantic love, which some might dismiss as sentimental and commonplace, or as basically selfish, has the mark of authentic love—a capacity for ignoring empirical characteristics (hence it is said to be blind). But in various personal relationships which we do not see as exemplifying romantic love we find indefeasible fidelity—love unaffected by illness, loss of beauty, or psychic breakdown in the one who is loved. And even in the public world traces of love in its strangeness can be seen. Care is taken of those hopelessly ruined by alcohol and drugs, and ways are sought of bringing back into the common life even those who have committed terrible crimes.

Love of this sort is often called *agape*. It was scarcely known in the ancient world, where love meant either *eros* or *philia*, both discriminating and exclusive. The attitudes of antiquity were manifest in acceptance of slavery, contempt for barbarians, and subordination of women. *Eros* and *philia* in their most generous forms were educational, bestowed where excellence remained to be actualized but never going so far as to disregard natural potentialities. *Agape* has its main historical roots in Christianity, in the faith that God committed himself to the cause of humanity in spite of human guilt and degradation. In forgiving man he sanctified him, bestowing on him a dignity—a claim on love—that man in his perversity had discarded. Love was commanded by the example and warranted by the transforming power of divine mercy.

As a deliberate act, love is humanly impossible. A person cannot will into existence love for another person or for humankind. For almost all of us, there are some who inspire aversion or hatred and many others to whom we are indifferent. Trying to love everyone, or even just one person in particular, is apt to eventuate only in unconscious hypocrisy. Although love is a power of discernment, there are no natural faculties and no techniques which make it attainable at will. As an insight into destinies it is, like destiny itself, given.

It is possible, however, to act in accordance with the requirements of love even when love in its fullness is not present. At best, this manifests only a fragmentary love and often not even that. But it is far from morally worthless. It is a way of acknowledging the authority of love and of obeying its commands. It is a kind of emulation.

In essence, it is a suspension of judgment. The sick, the insane, and the guilty are cared for even when doing this promises nothing for society or even for the one receiving care. It is recognized that our judgments of human beings, whether medical, psychiatric, or moral, and whether professional or personal, can never be complete and final. However much is known about a human being, individually and generically, he is never known finally and completely. And this is not merely because further scraps of evidence may always be found. The evidence possessed is invariably equivocal, subject to differing interpretations. Histories and biographies have to be recurrently rewritten. Today, authors of new interpretations often rely on theories, such as Marxism or psychoanalysis, which have reasonable grounds and help bring human realities to light. But none of these theories is demonstrable, none independent of philosophical views which the whole history of philosophy shows to be unstable and objectively uncertain. None makes a particular human being fully comprehensible.

Suspending judgment means adopting a posture of receptivity. Others are granted room for manifesting themselves in unforeseen and unforeseeable ways. This reveals the nature of love. In its fullness it is a joyful and uncalculated receptivity. In its fragmentary, or emulative, form it is disciplined receptivity. In both cases, others are approached with no absolutely decided prior expectations.

Love is receptivity not only in relation to persons but in

relation to transcendence as well. Suspension of judgment is called for not only by the mystery of a human being seen as a distinct and separate entity but also by the mystery of a human being in relation to transcendence. The origins of destiny are in transcendence. The nature and significance of every life are decided beyond the realms of rational investigation and definitive knowledge. Personal relationships therefore assume their most substantial forms when mediated by temporal signs of transcendence—religious and literary symbols, philosophical ideas, works of beauty, acts of moral resolution. Receptivity to others, or love, is not a relationship merely with finite individuals. It is a relationship with the truth—the Logos, which is human destiny understood as the order and meaning of all reality.

It is apparent, finally, that love is receptivity in relation not only to others and transcendence but also to oneself—to one's own destiny. Destiny illuminated by love is understood in its essential universality. But love is not in conflict with selfhood. It is a state of accessibility to a destiny that is personal as nothing else is, even though it is not an exclusive personal possession.

All of this may be clearer if love is seen in the form of communication. If personal relationships have their substance in mediating signs of transcendence, then love in its earthly imperfection must ordinarily be a search for those signs. It must take the form of common inquiry, of serious and probing communication. In sharing ultimate truth, even if that means sharing nothing more than the Socratic ignorance in which truth is not known but is sensed and sought, we enter into relations simultaneously with persons and with transcendence. And affirming ourselves as inquirers concerned ultimately with transcendence, selfhood too is discovered. Love cannot be fully expressed without speaking and listening of a kind that constitute openness toward transcendence. Nor can a personal destiny be worked out otherwise. If love is the power of understanding the world as a theatre for the fulfillment of destinies, communication is the cultivation and application of that power.

Communication may, then, assume the form of a search for the destined, or necessary, action. The realization of what one must do, like every realization of destiny, can be only an occasional and ephemeral experience. Neither an individual nor a society can act steadily under an imperative of necessity. But an individual can resolve to act only after efforts have been made to discover such an imperative. And a society can be organized so that action is conditional on inquiring communication.

Here political implications begin to emerge. The true political art consists in seeking and living human destiny in a communal fashion. We shall return to this matter after exploring the world in which the true political art has to be carried on—the world created by fate.

3

MAN AGAINST NATURE

IT IS A MAJOR premise of modern culture that human afflictions are due primarily to nature, not to humankind. The task before us is therefore that of subduing nature. This premise sustains our confidence in human will and power. It absolves human beings themselves from responsibility for creating the tragedies of history and makes it possible to believe that with the growth of their industrial prowess life will improve. It makes it also possible to believe that the extension of human power need not be over human beings. Nature will be governed by a spontaneously cooperative human race.

Marxism is illustrative. The meaning of history is held to lie in the conquest of nature. Human beings are not divided primarily by defects in their own character; the hatreds of class for class and of nation for nation derive ultimately from the material scarcities that make poverty for the vast majority inevitable and by the necessity, if these scarcities are to be overcome, for the kind of ruthless mass mobilization which capitalism (fulfilling its historical function) carries out. Once nature has been brought under control, the human situation will be transformed. It will be possible, even necessary, for human beings to work and live cooperatively. Class conflict will melt away and with it national rivalries and coercive government.

Marxism is only a persuasive and insurrectionary version

of the modern political faith. Most Americans and Europeans
have for a long time assumed that advancing industrialism
will eventually bring happiness and social harmony. A few
have come to question the advantages of continuous and un-
limited economic growth but they are dissenters from a
common faith. The controversies between left and right, between intellectuals and business executives, may cause us to
forget how much binds them together. The two sides often
differ as to how and for what ends industrial power should
be managed. But seldom do they dispute with one another
the beneficence of industrial power in itself. Both assume
that industrial and human progress are broadly coincident.
Marxism appeals to many because of its intellectual force and
its rebellious cast. In a certain way, however, it plays a har-
monizing role. It expresses the distaste many feel for the business ethos and capitalist culture while permitting unreserved
acceptance of the basic assumptions of industrial civilization.

Enthrallment with industrial progress is understandable,
for it is difficult not to think that industrialization is a necessary stage in human destiny. Nature threatens humanity in
a variety of ways, and it is worse than idle to dream of a life
of pastoral peace, innocent of technology and untouched by
industrial organization. Nevertheless, the value of technological and industrial development depends on what it is governed by—whether by will or by destiny.

The idea of destiny implies an underlying harmony of
man and nature. If a destiny is transcendentally given, it must
be naturally possible. This implies that in acting upon nature human beings should not aim at mastery, in order to
use nature as they please, but should strive rather to elicit the
basic accord which an understanding of destiny and of natural potentialities would reveal. This would mean abstaining
from efforts to make nature merely the servant of pride and
physical pleasure. In overcoming the hostility of nature, the
truth of nature itself would be brought forth.

Our opposition to nature is so habitual that talk of our
underlying harmony with nature is bound to seem implausible. Art and literature, however, indicate that such talk is

not untrue. A painting by Matisse is a vivid intimation of a paradise found at the core of being—a paradise gained neither, as in pastoral dreams, by abstinence from action nor, as in capitalist and Marxist dreams, by a triumph of will. A Beethoven symphony arouses our consciousness of an order of things not grounded in pristine nature or industrial artifice but in destiny. What we need from artists, composers, and writers is above all for them to awaken us to this order. The ugliness wrought by industrialism is not merely unpleasant. It is a sign of the violence we have done to nature and it tends to stifle the sense of reality needed for subordinating industrial power to destiny.

Distant though it may be from typical attitudes of the present day, the idea of the ultimate consonance of humankind and nature is one of the major themes in the philosophical and religious traditions of the West. In the philosophies of Plato and Aristotle the supreme task of a human being is to ascend intellectually to ultimate being, to apprehend the order governing at once the human and natural universe. Destiny is fulfilled in the discovery of cosmic harmony. This theme has been reiterated in various ways throughout the history of thought. It has been no less prominent in the history of religious insight. For the ancient Hebrews the physical universe reflected the purposes of the omnipotent Creator who brought forth humanity as well as nature. This faith, against the powerful opposition of Gnostic Christians, was incorporated in orthodox Christianity. In the Christian faith the physical universe is dignified not only by its origins in the creative act of God but also by the Incarnation. In the Gospel of John physical realities like bread, wine, and water are luminous symbols of spiritual realities.

Even death, according to this consensus, does not necessarily signify the defeat of man by nature. For both Socrates and Paul and for Plato as for Augustine, death could be, rather than a final blow dealt by fateful nature, an event within a personal destiny.

To undertake the conquest of nature is to misunderstand

at the same time nature and human power. Nature is not a totality of things that can be surveyed and comprehended. We cannot, as Kant shows, reach a beginning point in time, an outermost boundary in space, or an indivisible unit which enables us to declare that all is known. But since our knowledge is essentially incomplete, our actions are necessarily taken in partial ignorance. Even in principle we cannot foresee all consequences. Hence the unpleasant surprises attending the progress of industrialization—foul air, disintegrating cities, pervasive poisons. These are not accidents of a sort that we can learn to avoid. Insofar as industrialism aims at mastering nature, it is bound to fail. This is not because of any particular circumstance, such as burgeoning population. Perhaps no particular problem will prove insoluble. But there will be no end of problems, for every solution will create new ones.

The pride of industrial civilization, in the camps of capitalism and Marxism alike, renders us insensitive to these limits. Engaged in mastering nature, we fail to see the truth of nature; possessing unprecedented industrial power, we do not perceive our weakness; aspiring to command, we are unreceptive. The result is that nature, and our devices for mastering nature, assume the form of fate. Physical reality and the industrial order take on vast and threatening proportions.

Illustrative is the disorderly and unmanageable character of economic systems. An economic system is a set of institutions organized to control the material world. In our determination to be masters of that world, we persistently tell ourselves that the derangements afflicting the economic system— inflation, unemployment, and the like—will be not only cured but permanently precluded. Economic systems will in time be orderly and manageable. We are encouraged by representatives of every ideology to believe this. For socialists, order and control will come with the assertion of collective responsibility; for liberals, economic disharmonies will be eliminated as we become more adept in the use of ad hoc political correctives; for conservatives, economic systems are naturally harmonious and require only that governments protect property and peace and resist the mischievous schemes of altruists and reformers. But historical evidence lends little support to the faith in eventual economic harmony. Socialist governments, liberal governments, and free markets have none of them reconciled the working of economic mechanisms with the highest human values. In the aftermath of the depression of 1929 it was assumed that such an experience would never be repeated. Probably it will not. But that is mainly because historical experiences are rarely if ever repeated. The novel disorders afflicting economic life half-a-century after the Great Depression indicate that we have learned neither to control our economic systems in accordance with socialist or liberal designs nor to elicit the natural harmony envisioned by conservatives.

To say that we cannot understand and control an economic system as we might a well-designed machine is not to say that we can do nothing at all. Particular evils, such as unemployment, may be mitigated or removed. But economic systems are made up of human beings—beings who are both mysterious and refractory. Moreover, they are managed by human beings—beings imperfect in understanding and good will alike. The assumption that reliable economic harmony simply awaits a degree of further knowledge or the coming into power of a particular group or class depends for its plausibility on forgetting certain human characteristics.

A consequence of such forgetfulness is that governments grow in size, power, and pretensions, but not in effectiveness. The ethos of mastery inspires political leaders to claim the ability, and the commensurate powers, for managing the economic system. Government becomes large in size and efficient in spirit. But claims and expectations are rarely matched by results. Governments in this way become contemptible. Large and ambitious, they are also uncomprehending and ineffective.

Thus is presented the spectacle of fated government. Political leaders are prevented by the prevailing dedication to efficiency from gaining or evoking a sense of destiny. Instead, they obscure harsh realities and their own ineptitude by renewing the rhetoric of mastery. History unfolds in the dynamism of economic institutions and phenomena that are out of control. That those primarily responsible are moved by forces they cannot understand or direct becomes apparent to a cynical populace.

The irony of fate, that an inhuman world is produced by the utmost assertion of human will, is sharply etched in the industrial nations. Some of the most fateful conditions, those dwarfing and paralyzing individuals, are but mirrors of the human qualities cultivated and admired by industrial cultures. The vastness of national and global economic systems, for example, and the immensity of manufacturing and financial organizations—these but reflect the sweep of human intelligence and power. The same is true of characteristics other than size. The complexity and technicality which render many matters that are properly of common concern incomprehensible to the public derive from the subtlety and refinement of technological intelligence. We have in some ways created the world we intended to create, but that world turns out to be strange and inhospitable—human in source but not in character.

An ambiguity we have noted in the very concept of fate illuminates our situation. Fate seems incalculable and capricious. Otherwise we would not feel so vulnerable before it. Yet it comes upon us as something impersonal, implacable, unvarying—hence, in principle, rationally comprehensible. Both impressions are accurate, at least regarding the fate of people in industrial societies. In its totality it is irrational, bearing little relationship to genuine human needs and largely exempt from reasoned control. In its inner structure, however, it exhibits an extreme of rationality. The irony of fate takes the form of comprehensive irrationality characterized by highly-developed but circumscribed rationality. This paradox is at the center of Marxist interest, where it becomes a contradiction to be resolved by action.

We need not speculate, however, in order to become aware of the fate that has come upon us from our efforts at conquering nature. We need only look around us. Western nations have been engaged now for several generations in intensive efforts to establish human sovereignty over the physical universe. Yet that universe at present lies about us alien and threatening. The fateful effects of human self-assertion in its most ambitious and successful form, industrialization, are palpably manifest in the physical environment.

FATE AND THE EARTH

The quality of the environment does not concern us merely as physical beings. The earth is a setting for spiritual, not simply biological, life.

Both Hebrews and Greeks in ancient times envisioned the physical and the spiritual as one and undivided. Hence they thought of human life in even its exalted forms as having an appropriate physical setting, a setting that may be referred to simply as "the earth." In the Old Testament, "the earth is the Lord's and the fullness thereof." Through the earth humanity is related to the Creator, whose faithfulness "reaches unto the clouds," whose righteousness is "like the great mountains," whose "way is in the sea."[1] Upon the earth humanity has access to its destiny and Job can say, "Speak to the earth and it shall teach thee."[2]

For the peoples of ancient Greece, the *polis* provided a uniquely suitable sphere for the realization of destinies. The *polis* was not a purely natural setting but neither was it purely artificial. With its temples, dwellings, and fortifications it provided a visibly human environment; but unlike the modern city, it was small, unpaved, and close to the countryside. Many citizens were farmers and much of life even inside the city was carried on out-of-doors. The Athenian Assembly met on an open hillside; judicial and commercial proceedings were often conducted in unsheltered public places; philosophical inquiries were pursued in the sunlight of the agora. The earthliness of the *polis* was movingly evoked by Alfred Zimmern when he wrote of how "the Athenian had loved the Acropolis rock while it was still rough and unlevelled, when the sun, peeping over Hymettus, found only ruddy crags and rude Pelasgian blocks to illumine," and of how he loved it even more "when its marble temples caught the first gleam of the morning or stood out, in the dignity of perfect line, against a flaming sunset over the mountains to the West."[3]

The Athenian Acropolis, with its marble temples, exemplifies the concept of the earth: neither untouched by humanity nor molded in every detail; rather, nature understood as a scene fitted for the enactment of destinies and thus crowned with emblems of humanity and its relationship with transcendence. Our situation in the twentieth century is disquieting because the earth, thus defined, has largely disappeared from the lives of most of us.

As I have already indicated, the state of the earth reflects our inherent inability to comprehend the natural world as a totality. We can of course scientifically understand limited segments of the physical universe, and accordingly we can shape limited areas of the earth in conformity with prior design. We can build beautiful parks and civic centers. But the physical universe as a whole evades our understanding, and accordingly the physical environment evades our control. This is exemplified in the squalor and desolation of many cities in the wealthiest nations. This example, however, points to another aspect of the earth we seek to master and, correspondingly, to another facet of our finitude.

Physical realities cannot be cleanly distinguished from psychological, social, and other realities. Controlling physical realities thus depends on understanding a wide range of human realities. The squalor and desolation of cities reflects something far more ominous than the inherent limits of physical science: a spiritual and political failure. As destined lives have an appropriate physical setting in "the earth," so fated lives are apt to be carried on and made visibly manifest in a ravaged earth. To master the earth we would have to comprehend in addition to the natural world the spiritual world as well.

The state of the earth reflects not only our inability to do this, however. It also reflects the motives which accompany this inability. These motives all are perverse, if judged by the standard of receptivity. All are forms of the will to mastery. That will is evident as commercial avarice (countrysides spoiled by billboards and shopping centers), as a disposition to reduce the earth to a mere store of raw materials (hillsides scarred by timber and mining entrepreneurs), utilitarianism indifferent to visible grace and meaning (rows of houses distinguished only by trivial stylistic variations). The physical world might serve us today as a moral mirror.

Specific conditions do not need to be drawn to anyone's attention. The significance of some of these conditions, however, may deserve brief comment.

Ugliness

Our insensitivity to destiny is manifest in the ugliness that pervades the industrial world. A great art critic argues that beauty, by facilitating the act of perception, instills a consciousness of power.[4] Ugliness, conversely, brings feelings of weakness. If beauty indicates an ontological harmony that constitutes a possibility and a call to live a certain life, then ugliness testifies to an encirclement by fate. A human race bent on industrial mastery necessarily cares little for beauty, and the unsightly surroundings it creates say nothing to us of destiny and confirm the state of mind in which they originate.

Pollution

An elemental and telling sign of our relationship to the earth can be seen in the dirt and poison that abound in our air, water, and food. Our physical surroundings are not altogether supportive even of life, to say nothing of destiny. This is because contaminating the environment is sometimes difficult to avoid and often profitable. Finitude and avarice conspire together, which should warn us against thinking that a merely healthful earth, in an industrial age, is readily attainable. Some pollution no doubt is inevitable. But how near can we come to suffering no more than that? Destiny provides the form for life and, hence, as we abandon our concern for destiny we necessarily lose our ability to care for life. This is at least one source of the irony that we are surrounded by miracles of industrial mastery but often lack good water and healthful air.

Instability

One way in which our contact with the earth has been attenuated is simply through the loss of environmental stability. Even if our surroundings were beautiful and healthful, it would be disturbing for them to be, as they are, continually and unpredictably changing. Human beings need things around them that are not merely familiar but that are resonant with voices from the past. They particularly need this for living a destiny, which involves gathering up and carrying forward a personal and social history. Even those who escape the tides of mobility engulfing modern populations are apt to be deprived of a stable environment today. A person who has spent a lifetime in one place may experience, year after year, the uneasiness of the newcomer. It is the irony of fate that if mastery is emphatically asserted, the limits of mastery are emphatically experienced. Hence our deprivation—in an age when the industrial order exhibits the human capacity for carrying out large and dramatic undertakings—of so elemental a value as a firm and tranquil earth.

It is noteworthy how small a part untamed nature has in the contemporary fate of the Western world. Earthquakes, storms, and droughts are among the slighter dangers. It is the manmade environment—unsightly, unhealthful, and unstable—that threatens us. The unsubdued earth perhaps threatens us as much by its inaccessibility as by its upheavals. Many human beings today have hardly any contact with unspoiled nature—as severe and elemental a deprivation as that of environmental stability. We are not alienated from nature because we are human and nature is not, but because we have rendered nature perversely human.

One thing that might be said in defense of industrial peoples is that they have not tried to make the natural world congenial but rather to rise above it. They have sought liberation. How far they have succeeded may be judged by how far they have freed themselves from the kind of enslavement nature has long imposed, that of toil.

FATE AND TOIL

Toil is the mythical curse pronounced upon man for disobeying God. "In the sweat of thy face," Adam is told after unlawfully acquiring knowledge of good and evil, "shalt thou eat bread till thou return unto the ground."[5] This can easily be read in terms of fate and destiny. Toil is humanity's fate. Human beings perversely claim sovereignty over their lives and being; this is symbolized by Adam eating fruit from the forbidden tree. The consequence (symbolized as Adam's expulsion from the Garden of Eden) is that human beings lose consciousness of their destinies and fall into subjection to the demands of mere physical existence.

It is surprising how well this myth fits our present circumstances in spite of the transformations brought about by industrialism. Toil in the industrial age is far different from toil in earlier ages and is far more highly rewarded. It still, however, dominates our lives. Far from invalidating the biblical myth, industrial societies have enriched and confirmed it.

This is brought out with great dramatic force, and with full regard for the irony of the situation, in the writings of Marx and of followers such as Herbert Marcuse. In asserting mastery over the physical world—a mastery which would supposedly bring liberation from toil—humankind created a work-system which actually enslaved it. With the industrial revolution workers found themselves, due to the irresistible imperatives of their jobs, alienated from the earth (from nature and its diurnal and seasonal tempos), from fellow-workers (since relations among workers are governed by the demands of mass production, rather than vice versa), from the products of work (not chosen or designed by the workers), and in these ways alienated from themselves. In a word, workers were denied the opportunity of living a human destiny. Marx saw capitalism as a fated work-system, robbing the workers not just of health and satisfaction but of their very being. What made capitalism intolerable for Marx was its perversion of the power accessible to the human race through technology. From the perspective of the distant future, Marx believed this perversion could be seen as a necessary stage in the full unfoldment of human creative powers. From the perspective of his own time, however, it exhibited the irony of nature transformed into fate by an assertion of human command.

Some of Marx's expectations, of course, have been falsified. The proletarian misery so carefully and bitterly delineated in *Capital* has not grown worse, as Marx thought it would. It is now experienced by relatively few, mainly by so-far unassimilated racial minorities. The work done by the lower classes is not, on the whole, nearly so destructive of elementary decencies as it was in Marx's day.

To suppose that Marx's view of industrialized work has thus been rendered wholly irrelevant, however, would be to misunderstand Marx, the character of work in our own time, or both. The point of Marx's critique was not that industrialized work was onerous and unremunerative. The point was that it deprived workers of their humanity. That it did this in part through being onerous and unremunerative was incidental. Marx did not very clearly foresee that toil might be lightened and wages raised to such a degree that workers would more or less willingly subject themselves to the degradations of toil. The fact that this has happened invalidates many of the particulars of Marx's analysis. But it does not invalidate its main purport.

The work-systems of the Western nations are no longer

oppressive, by and large, but they still are fateful. The essence of toil is that its demands do not represent the true being of those who must meet them. Toil is fate in the form of work. As seen in chapter 1, fate can be pleasurable and even seductive, enticing people to acquiesce in order to escape the uncertainties and responsibilities of selfhood. Work destructive of selfhood is toil even if it is pleasurable and seductive. Work which hinders one in perceiving and responding to the demands of one's own destined life is fateful regardless of how willingly it is done. Industrialization has in a variety of ways alleviated the misery of toil but it has not eliminated toil. Further, if it has lessened its power in some ways, say, by limiting the number of hours it can claim from daily life, it has magnified its power in other ways. Recreation and comfort contribute no more to destiny than do toil and misery. But by rendering fate more attractive they may serve, as Rousseau said was done by the arts and sciences, as garlands of flowers concealing our chains.

The fatefulness of modern work can be seen in the ways it reflects the blindness of pride. In its most commonly noted characteristic, the mechanization of the worker, for example, it reflects blindness to the mystery and plenitude of being. It partakes of the deadly objectification inherent in the will to mastery. It does this not only in factories but in almost all organizations, and thus it affects all classes. Treated as things of the same order as machines and raw materials, human beings are reduced not merely to nature but to nature that has itself been reduced to causal relationships. Fate appears as an efficient but humanly destructive system of oversimplification.

Modern work reflects blindness also to the perversity of human beings. Industrialization has excited and empowered human selfishness. Amplifying avarice and ambition it has brought work to the service of ignoble ends. This was not fully anticipated in the early years of industrialism. Technology and machinery seem like products of pure intelligence, unaffected by evil and lending themselves to use in the public interest. Supporters of capitalism expected that selfishness would be nullified by the market, supporters of communism expected it to disappear once capitalism was eliminated. On both sides these expectations led to unchecked power—in the hands of capitalists or of public functionaries—and on both sides they have proven thoroughly delusory. America has shown that industrial power can excite the thirst for money and power to such a degree that daily life is cast largely as an affair of making, advertising, and consuming material goods, many of them trivial, some of them harmful. The Soviet Union has shown that industrial power can be an effective instrument of despotism. In both systems work is fateful because it is severed from the true ends of life, from destiny.

Our obliviousness of destiny in our lives of work is evident in our neglect of two long-standing concepts that fuse considerations of destiny and work. These are the concepts of vocation and of leisure. Both deserve our attention.

A vocation is a type of work in which one sees possibilities of discovering and living a destiny. The vocational character of work may be manifest immanently by its fulfillment of personal potentialities and transcendentally by its being experienced as something one is called upon to do. Every human being has a moral right to a vocation, even though there will probably never be any practical way in which it can be made a legal right as well. The reason underlying this right is not that destiny is necessarily inaccessible without a vocation; someone might discover his destiny in struggling against confining or meaningless work. It is rather that a human being is distinguished from a material thing or an animal by the capacity for fulfilling a vocation. Hence a society careless of vocations is careless of persons and submissive to fate.

It is difficult, however, to think of a modern society—capitalist, socialist, or communist—that is not careless of vocations. Despite the fashion of "vocational counselling," nations today are concerned above all with production and distribution. This is understandable in view of the poverty of most nations and of some groups within even the wealthiest nations. It is not wholly defensible, however. Nations that are far from poor are not merely concerned, but are preoccupied, with production and distribution. One can see this as a sign both of a powerful acquisitive impulse arising out of the ethos of mastery and of an insensitivity to the idea of destiny. Governments, businesses, and unions have given little serious consideration to the idea of using our unprecedented wealth in order to reshape work and, thus, to explore the meaning of our humanity in ways impossible in earlier and poorer ages.

We are no less neglectful of leisure, although we perhaps do not intend to be. Leisure is freedom for serious and demanding activity outside the bounds of work. Leisure is not recreation, for recreation is recuperation from work and is essentially a requirement of work. Leisure, as freedom from the constraints of work, is freedom also from the need for recuperation. As for the kind of activity appropriate to leisure, any activity is appropriate that is called for by one's destiny but not by one's work. Above all, leisure is for reflection—for clarifying one's situation and purposes.

To enjoy leisure is to realize the joy of life that is free from toil. Someone with a perfect vocation—someone with work exactly matching his destiny and therefore not burdened with toil—would have no need for leisure. But hardly anyone has a perfect vocation, for hardly anyone is so sheltered from the winds of fate. Leisure is a hedge against fate.

Our neglect of leisure is manifest in the vast resources we devote to recreation—to entertainment and sports, to activities we appropriately term "diversions." There are various reasons for our devotion to recreation: recreation depends on equipment and hence is a far greater source of profits than is leisure; recreation is politically safe, while leisure may give rise to unorthodox or rebellious thoughts; recreation is easy, whereas leisure is demanding, and we have defined liberty as doing what we please. But a recreational society, in contrast with its appearance and with the impression it is likely to have of itself, is apt also to be a toilsome society. Only through toil can it provide its members with opportunities to be serious, that is, to set distant ends and to submit to discipline, and only through toil can it create the wealth that recreation requires.

The irony of our situation, that we possess a high degree of technological mastery but ignore vocations and lack leisure, can be explained in part as the price of mastery. Devoting ourselves to technology and industry, we have had to forget much else. It can be explained in part also by the extreme difficulties we would encounter in remembering all we have forgotten. The dream of mastery, and its embodiment in technology and industry, have not come in a light and ephemeral moment in the history of Western man. We could not cease toiling without transforming our relations with nature.

Although work remains under the primal curse, toilsome, one might assume that the wealth we create balances the scales. Life in the West is now far longer, more secure, more comfortable, and more abundantly endowed with opportunities than ever before. Nothing, however, shows more emphatically the fatefulness of our relations with the physical universe than the fact that even our wealth, so spectacular and in some ways beneficial, stands over us as fate.

FATE AND WEALTH

Some of the fateful characteristics of modern wealth have been frequently noted—that it is, for example, often as questionable in utility as it is vast in quantity. Much of it serves trivial or destructive ends, enhancing mere convenience or comfort, or, less than that, fulfilling functions that cannot be eliminated in present circumstances but that do not amplify our lives (such as automobiles as mere necessities of suburban existence). Much of the wealth of the industrial nations takes the form of weapons of annihilation. At the same time we are often without elemental values such as reliably wholesome food and pure air.

That modern wealth is mostly owned and controlled by minorities is another fateful characteristic and a commonplace of social criticism. The fatefulness of this condition, however, is commonly minimized by critics, for supposedly it can be readily overcome. Ownership and control can be taken from minorities and given to the public. But it is hard to see how this is possible. The development and application of technology and the organization of industry require the entrepreneurial initiative and managerial authority of minorities, and for these minorities to be civil servants rather than private individuals makes little difference. "Public ownership" is a beguiling but, present experience strongly suggests, meaningless phrase.

Even if wealth could be transferred from the few to the many, moreover, it is far from clear that this would eliminate the fated qualities of wealth. Minority ascendancy is perhaps only the most conspicuous sign, not the basic cause, of our deranged relationships with our wealth. This is suggested by the Marxist principle that the major acts of the ascendant minorities—capitalists—are as relentlessly determined by the laws of economic development as are the movements of any other segment of society. It is suggested, too, by conditions on which a mere redistribution of wealth would seem to have little bearing.

Modern wealth, for example, is thoroughly alien. We have created much, in our drive to mastery, but have taken possession of little. The things we own are too numerous for us to know and adequately appreciate as individual possessions; they are frequently not owned for very long or even, free of debt, owned at all; they are ordinarily made by machines and do not, like works of craftsmanship, embody the personality of a maker; they exist in numberless duplicates, and this too hinders close identification of owner and thing; and they are often intricately mechanical, largely incomprehensible to the owner, and thus necessarily left to the care of specialists. Modern possessions are stubbornly impersonal, as though they belong, in defiance of all legal titles, to society at large. Manifesting in every detail human technological intelligence and industrial genius, they resist personal appropriation. In this way they are aspects of a physical universe that is alien even though—or, more accurately, because—we have created it.

Although the things making up our wealth are many of them alien, to resist their proliferation is difficult. Collectively, we are forced to keep on producing and consuming. Otherwise, industries will collapse, jobs will be lost, and the whole society will be faced with hardship. In order to have the things we need, seemingly we must make and acquire much that we do not need.

Independence is difficult personally as well as collectively. It is not practicable to live within a modern industrial society and yet to live independently of the material wealth it produces. Such wealth is not simply a set of objects that may be appropriated or spurned. It constitutes the structure of daily existence. One cannot work and rest and establish enduring relationships without participating in that structure. This means, moreover, beyond acquiring the instrumentalities which that structure provides, accepting the values which it sanctions. We are enticed continually from every side not merely to acquiesce in the life that industrialism provides but to enjoy it. Even those antagonistic to advertising are not likely to remain unaffected by the impression it so diligently tries to create: that the world is filled with commodities in which we can find both satisfaction and often some kind of personal renewal as well.

It would be an oversimplification, however, to suggest that the fateful impact of wealth on our values comes about mainly by our coming to rely on material goods. It is not only materialism which testifies to our subjugation, but also anomie. Modern wealth instills in each one a consciousness of being surrounded by opportunities—for enjoyment, for travel, for personal development, for almost anything that is fancied. But these opportunities are far too numerous and expensive to be fully enjoyed and they are too random to sustain any order in the process of enjoyment. Unguided by a sense of destiny, either from within or from society, one does not know which opportunities to use and may have the disquieting feeling either of living arbitrarily or of being strangely immobilized on the very boundaries of happiness. Even someone rich enough to respond to the most alluring of the possibilities that beckon may be overcome by an avidity to enjoy and accomplish everything and consequently lose the instinct for order and limits that is grounded in a sense of destiny.

Some argue that the chief problem before us is not wealth but poverty. Discussions of the moral perils of prosperity are seen as merely one of the pastimes of privileged minorities. But I suggest that the problem of poverty today is an aspect of the problem of wealth. The continuance of deep poverty in the midst of unprecedented wealth reflects the fated character of that wealth, that it is not pliant to humane purposes. Poverty today is in some ways worse for the poor themselves than it has ever been, at least within the industrialized societies. Now it cannot be endured as the lot of everyone and is not likely to be endured, given the power of the prevailing secularism, as one of the ordeals in which destiny is forged. It is exceptional and without justification in terms of any public philosophy. At the same time, there is practically no prospect at all of its ever being eliminated, even within the wealthiest nations. The majority has tasted prosperity and thirsts for more. Only minorities are poor, and these for the most part are powerless, without means of exacting either justice or favors. Modern wealth is a fate in one way for those who have access to it, in another way for those who do not.

Our very concept of wealth displays the urge to command. Wealth, we assume, is composed of things made, owned, and used. It is nature subjected to will. Acting on this concept, we have brought into existence a quantity of goods many times greater than humankind has ever before had at its disposal. In their totality, however, these goods ironically evade our control and in that sense weaken and impoverish us.

When wealth takes the form of fate, it contributes to the rise of the political phenomenon noted earlier in this chapter: government cast as a servant of fate and in that role magnified and disabled. It is a central tenet of the liberal creed that through humanitarian politics and the wise employment of governmental power we can subordinate wealth to the highest moral laws and human ends. Through politics, supposedly, human beings can transcend their fateful existence as producers and consumers of wealth. Looking to American experience, we may grant that the liberal faith is not wholly in error. People are capable of some consideration, and of politically effective consideration, for the needs of all. But American experience also indicates limits upon the validity of the liberal creed. Where most members of a society devote themselves primarily to acquiring and keeping wealth, politics and government will be used primarily to serve these ends. Hence, two generations of economic reform in the United States have only given rise to a society in which almost everyone, rather than a privileged few, is able to lose himself in production and consumption. Such egalitarianism, moreover, responded not just to moral but to economic imperatives. An impoverished populace is incompatible with a vital market.

Wealth in another way contributes to the stupefaction of government. Its fateful dynamics are a major source of the disorderly and unmanageable character of economic systems. Inflation, for example, would not be as serious as it is apart from the acquisitiveness motivating all classes. This is easily put in Marxist terms. Marx tried to overcome economic disorder and political incapacity by discovering the laws governing the dynamics of industrial wealth. But for Marx knowledge of these laws would provide a basis for reasserting human will. This means reinforcing fate. We can infer, and experience so far indicates, that socialist governments will be no less fated—distended, uncomprehending, ineffective—than liberal governments have been.

The first prerequisite for subordinating industrial power to human need is a new concept of wealth. The present concept is not wholly wrong. It avoids any idealization of pristine nature and envisions all non-human physical reality as properly attendant on humanity. It sees this state, however, as secured primarily by human will. In this way it obscures the truth that authentic wealth is not created. The sense of destiny, especially when it comes to us through natural and artistic beauty, shows us the entire physical universe as wealth—not in its idyllic outer aspect, but in its inner being. Action on the physical universe, through technology and industry, serves humanity in the measure that it is guided by this insight, uncovering the basic accord between humanity and nature. But so far as action is motivated by the urge to command, it falls under those illusions concerning nature and humanity that give rise to fate and thus generate wealth that is alien and threatening.

Adhering to a true concept of wealth—a concept presupposing not merely a different economic viewpoint but a different spiritual outlook from that of modern society—acting thus as midwives rather than creators, we might bring into existence a reborn earth. Paul expressed a clear intuition of such a possibility when he spoke of creation, which "groaneth and travaileth in pain together until now," being "delivered from the bondage of corruption."[6] Marx voiced a similar idea. He saw communism as producing "man in all the plenitude of his being, the wealthy man endowed with all the senses, as an enduring reality," and he delineated the prospect of "the accomplished union of man with nature, the veritable resurrection of nature."[7] But a reborn earth is not, as Marx thought, simply a product of the natural unfoldment of technological genius. It is the encircling harmony of humanity and nature brought to light in destinies. Technology must be employed within this encircling harmony if it is to call into being "the wealthy man" rather than the man of the present historical moment, one who is paradoxically impoverished by his wealth.

Nature is threatening in the forms we have given it—as an ugly and noxious environment, a burdensome work system, oppressive wealth. It is more than threatening in a form we have not given it and cannot in essence alter, that of death. Here the whole human effort to master nature comes to an unsuccessful end.

But is it an unsuccessful end? Modern man is fully cognizant of the denouement lying before him and does not appear greatly shaken. That the life we have here on earth is the only life we shall ever enjoy is axiomatic in modern consciousness; even Christians do not often take a stand against secularism on this ground. Most people, however, avow that the finality of death in no way weakens their belief in life or their fidelity to the altruistic morality that has for centuries been linked with the idea of personal immortality. Some assert that the value of life is enhanced by the prospect of its obliteration and that morals are purified by their separation from calculations of eternal reward. The modern sense of mortality seems free of cynicism and despair.

Does the nonchalant bearing of modern man before "the king of terrors" constitute a triumph of modern humanism, or is it a sign of superficiality that we make so little of the brutal ascendancy that nature will someday assert over each one of us? The question is not whether life without hope of immortality must be terrifying or unhappy. It need not be. Life has pleasures and joys that are not necessarily banished by our awareness of their evanescence. The question is not how we happen to feel before the prospect of complete extinction but what we should think. It is a question of logical implications. What is the meaning for life of the finality of death?

A great writer of modern times has devoted practically all of his work in one way or another to this question and has given an answer which, for me, is fully convincing. The writer is Dostoevsky. The answer may be summed up in the concept of demoralization. Dostoevsky saw modern man losing his Christian faith and in consequence facing, perhaps in criminal or revolutionary self-assertion, perhaps in dissipation and despair, the apparent certainty of complete personal annihilation. One cannot live in a truly human way without respect for others and respect for oneself, that is, without love. The comprehensive respect which is love, however, is dependent on faith in the immortality of the individual person. When that faith disappears the result is demoralization, a state ensuing upon a twofold loss: of morality and of morale.

The loss of morality which Dostoevsky foresaw can be characterized in terms of his well-known assertion that if death is final, "all is permitted." If every reality is at last completely extinguished and forgotten, if every act and event leads finally into oblivion, then it does not matter how one lives. Some, from native kindliness or a distaste for trouble, may continue to adhere to the old moral code. Others, however, differing in temperament or circumstances, may not. Given the axiom that death is final, what can be said to them? Will not death, annihilating the criminal and the tyrant, and obliterating at last every memory of their misdeeds, effectively clear the books? It is often said that people do not need to be lured or frightened by pictures of everlasting bliss or misery into behaving decently. Considering how indecently so many in our time have behaved, the validity of this contention is not evident. Dostoevsky's views are unfairly coarsened, however, if the issue is wholly reduced to one of eternal punishments and rewards. The issue in part is whether there is anything eternal at all. The moral devastation inherent in the belief that death is final is associated with the realization that if all realities and all that we value are destined to disappear and be forgotten, then even now they are enveloped in a cosmic, irresistible indifference. A criminal or a tyrant is only an ephemeral appearance on the face of everlasting darkness. The consequences of every deed will trickle into historical rivers and thence into a sea of total oblivion.

It must be remembered how much Judaic-Christian morality demands of us: not just decency in our relations with those around us but rather treatment of every person according to the principle that a human being is of measureless worth. Raskolnikov was not inconsiderate of relatives and friends. He was not, in the ordinary sense of the word, selfish nor was he unconcerned with the welfare of the human race. He merely was prepared to measure the worth of an old woman.

And why not, if death is final? Morality rests in two ways on faith in personal immortality. It rests on the faith that I myself, in spite of death, am accountable for my life: mortality is not impunity. It rests also on the faith that the human beings I encounter are not mere passing phenomena. Raskolnikov could tell himself that the old woman was of no use to society and hence of no value at all; and physically spent, she would soon be dead whether or not he killed her. A belief in personal immortality would have provided a different perspective, one not permitting the worth of a person to be measured by utilitarian or quantitative calculations.

Dostoevsky did not see the danger as solely that of unleashed selfishness, however. Those no longer in awe of eternity will not necessarily seek pleasure and advantage for themselves. On the contrary, they may try to redeem the world. And in their more grandiose and "unselfish" undertakings they may be at their most murderous—an idea to which recent experience lends sombre plausibility. Raskolnikov's ultimate aim—like Stalin's (assuming the sincerity of his Marxist professions)—was the happiness of all mankind.

The other aspect of demoralization, loss of morale, may be understood simply as radical discouragement before the prospect of personal extinction. If one's being is defined not merely by the past and present but by all that one is yet to become, if the meaning of the past is decided in the future, then if one is bound to become nothing, if the future is nothingness, then even one's past and present are nullified by mortality. Death does not wait at the end but reaches back and embraces the whole of life.

Loss of morale may also be understood, however, as resulting from the loss of morality. To be freed from all moral restraints does not place one in a state of glorious liberty. It threatens despair. If there is no reason for living in one way rather than another, life becomes a matter of whim and preference, without meaning. Morality is often spoken of as if it were merely a set of prohibitions which happen to be obligatory yet are in conflict with every form of happiness and satisfaction, aside perhaps from the satisfaction of doing what is right. But the truth is that morality is recognition of the significance of life in the form of imperatives of conduct. A life without such imperatives is without significance. Hence the issue for Dostoevsky was not merely how, in a universe ruled by death, we could live without scandalously misbehaving, but how we could live at all and not be overwhelmed by the absurdity of existence.

Morality, then, undergirds morale. But the converse also is true. When morale is lost, morality necessarily suffers. Those facing the apparent absurdity of existence will be less inclined than ever to adhere to the moral law. They may subside into peaceful but irresponsible apathy or they may seek self-forgetfulness and significance of life in fanaticism.

From here every road leads to tyranny. One motive is order. When voluntary restraint ceases to exist, forcible restraint must take its place. Another motive is renown. Those whose thirst for immortality is not quenched metaphysically may try to satisfy it politically. A contemporary psychiatrist sees in the life of Mao Tse-tung a quest for "revolutionary immortality."[8] Hitler designated his regime a "Thousand-Year Reich." The multitudes who must serve as the materials of such projects, all viewed as in the very nature of the universe fated for extinction, cannot arouse moral inhibitions in the tyrant any more than can the blocks of marble with which he builds architectural and sculptural memorials of his power.

Modern man assumes that in believing in the finality of death he is only facing facts. But while death is a fact, its finality is not. Like its counter-concept, personal immortality, it is faith and surmise. Hence a question concerning motives is in order. To assume that death means total extinction is no doubt sometimes an act of courage, an adherence in spite of all personal longing to what seems to be the truth. But it may be a less creditable act than that.

It may sometimes be an effort not to face a hard truth but to evade a disturbing one. Anticipation of eternal life is not a source of unalloyed comfort. The thought that there is no escaping from existence, or from the consequences of one's acts, gives life a disquieting seriousness. It precludes comfortable and unconcerned enjoyment of the present moment. Had this thought a larger place in modern consciousness it might greatly interfere with the lives we lead. The sense of mortality in modern man is allied with an unapologetic devotion to enjoyment.

The sense of mortality is allied also with pride. To deny the finality of death is to associate every person with a rationally impenetrable mystery. A being destined for eternal life cannot be totally accessible to rational investigation or deliberate management. Hence pride arouses resistance to the concept of personal immortality and inclines us to see human beings as objects and nothing more. But once human beings are seen as objects, as things that can be rationally comprehended and controlled, the question of personal immortality is settled. If human beings are purely objects then they must die wholly and conclusively. An object, however complex and fascinating it may be, exists by definition entirely in space and time and is therefore finite and mortal. Our certainty of the finality of death thus is not necessarily a reasoned conclusion or a compelling intuition. It may be only a postulate required by our aspiration to universal dominion. This is not to suggest that the logic linking the denial of personal immortality and the will to dominion is plain to our consciousness or that it is so simple and direct as my argument might suggest. I mean only to point to the probability of implicative relationships between a view of reality as comprehensively objective and a desire to bring reality under complete control. Assuming such relationships, however, then it is the irony of our fate that the quest for mastery has led us to accept premises that imply our complete annihilation.

We must bear in mind, therefore, that the defeat we face in having to die may not be a defeat inflicted by nature in itself but by nature transformed by human will into fate. Every human being has to die, but not every human being is fated to die. For some, death is destiny rather than fate. Although it is difficult to say exactly what this means, it is a matter of common experience. We all are aware of deaths, like those of Socrates and Jesus, that define and give meaning to life. But for those who have repudiated destiny and seek to dominate the physical universe, death comes as an annihilating blow of fate. It is nature's final and unanswerable rejoinder to our pride.

4

MAN AGAINST HUMANITY

PRIDE AND IDEALISM

THE EFFORT TO dominate nature brings about an incidental effort to dominate humanity. For nature to be controlled, human beings must be mobilized; factories exemplify this connection. Where all reliance is on will and action, however, the mobilization of human beings is unlikely to be merely incidental. For pride, it will be an end in itself. The supreme proof of mastery would be to direct the course of history.

The two motives of mastery, control of nature and control of humanity, often are so fused as to be indistinguishable. Probably few industrialists, for example, could demarcate and weigh them even by careful introspection. Not always, however, are they fused. Some human beings, typified by the engineer and inventor, are moved primarily by possibilities of commanding nature, whereas others, such as military and political leaders, are interested almost exclusively in commanding human beings. In similar fashion can events sometimes be distinguished. The settling of the North American continent in the nineteenth century was primarily an act of conquest over nature; the Indians were incidental victims. The Revolution of 1789 in France was an effort to direct the course of history.

In some ways domination of human beings parallels the domination of nature. It begins in a similar blindness on the part of the powerful: to the full reality of the entities they wish to control—now, ominously, human beings; to their own finitude and consequent vulnerability to results unanticipated in the initiation of their acts—results that may be especially startling when they originate with human beings; to their own imperfections and perversities—which may take on uglier shapes where humanity, rather than nature, is the antagonist; and to destiny. Beginning in a darkening of the understanding similar to that inherent in the effort to dominate nature, the effort to dominate humanity has broadly similar results. The object of power, now human rather than natural, imperfectly understood, and negligently or cruelly handled, evades control and is reconstituted as fate. Revolutions, unfolding as inspiration, then terror, and finally reaction, offer classic examples.

The parallel is not complete, however, and to assume that it is would obscure important aspects both of human relations and of our own times. Human beings are not approached in the same way as nature even when approached with the same masterful intent.

People are rarely so cynical that they desire, even if they could justify before others, undisguised mastery. Hence they usually strive not for the kind of domination that openly enslaves their fellow human beings but for the kind that is calculated to better their lives and even to set them free. Rousseau suggested a fusion of the will to domination and the will to liberation when he spoke of people being "forced to be free." Modern man has tried to impose on nature complete subservience, but he has dealt more considerately, if not more gently, with his fellow human beings: he has tried to shape their lives in accordance with exalted ideals. This is not merely a matter of convenient duplicity, although that is part of it. The power-seeking idealism of our age testifies to feelings of unfeigned solidarity.

The sovereign ideals for modern man have been those of the French Revolution: liberty, equality, and fraternity. The revolutions of the twentieth century have often appealed to a far more sophisticated analysis of history (that of Marx) than the revolutions of earlier times could call upon, but they have been inspired by the same ideals. The Soviet and Chinese Revolutions, whatever their actual results, have been carried out in the name of a free, equal, and fraternal life. It is not enslavement, then, that has been the characteristic aim of modern pride but the complete and final liquidation of enslavement.

This has given a particular poignancy to the irony of our fate. Freedom, equality, and fraternity are necessarily falsified when they become objects of a rational will. Human beings cannot forcibly be made to be free, equal, and fraternal, in spite of Rousseau. The effort to do so necessarily has results very different from those sought. Hence our fate has not merely been that we have fallen short of the ideals of the French Revolution but that we have often moved away from them in the very effort to approach them. Granted, there is probably more freedom, equality, and fraternity in the world today than there was in 1789. But this is not because we have established them in places, times, and ways of our own choosing. Like the God of the Israelites, revealed to those who did not seek Him, modern ideals have been given their most reliable social and political forms by peoples, such as the English, who have approached them warily. They have had a troubled history among more impassioned protagonists, such as the French, and have been grossly violated by their most intransigent champions, the Russians.

Such ironies fit the concept of irony framed in this essay. The ideals of liberty, equality, and fraternity can express a sense of destiny—of human beings as living under imperatives that render them irreducible to any coercive order (free), incomparable by the standards of any social hierarchy (equal), and ultimately at one (fraternal). Thus the revolutionary effort to direct history toward liberty, equality, and fraternity arose from a valid insight into the nature and requirements of our humanity. But the determination to fulfill this responsibility at places and times, and in ways, willed by man, has made fate overwhelming. The revolutionaries themselves have usually been swept away by the events they have set in motion. The ideals they have been implacably determined to enact have been more fully realized by more hesitant reformers. This does not mean that the efforts of revolutionaries have been fruitless. But they have not borne the fruits intended.

We are not concerned only with revolutionaries, however. The urge to mastery is omnipresent in modern society. Reformers have been more cautious than revolutionaries, but they have not been exemplars of humility. And although their efforts have on the whole been more successful than those of revolutionaries, those efforts have not been unattended by ironic reverses.

We should remember, too, that the urge to mastery does not always take political forms. The industrial revolution is no less striking a sign of our Promethean temper than the French Revolution. Here too idealism appears, although entrusted for enactment to the invisible hand of the market. Here too idealism suffers ironic failures. Our fate includes not only despotic hierarchies founded, as in Russia, for the sake of equality but also proletarian enslavement wrought, as in England, in the name of freedom of contract.

In order to be concise, we shall dwell on political idealism. But we are concerned with the overall plight of modern man: that he has come into conflict with his highest values in the very pursuit of those values. His idealism has brought him into conflict with his own humanity.

The political irony noted in the preceding chapter—governments that are large and activist, yet ineffective—becomes particularly sharp as a result of idealistic efforts at human domination. Programs designed to set people free, to reduce or nullify social and economic inequality, and to bring unity are almost certain to require massive and highly-centralized governmental institutions. At the same time they are likely to call into being, or at least to reinforce, that vast, unmanageable entity often called "the masses"—an unstructured and insensitive populace. The result is government that is large and pretentious but not very effective. Such government is disqualified by its very nature from realizing or evoking a sense of destiny. Its magnitude and helplessness are signs of its fated character.

These circumstances make for totalitarianism—government that throws off every limit in a desperate effort to gain control. But experience gives few indications that such efforts are likely to succeed. Although the totalitarian governments of our time have not failed in everything, they have failed to reach major goals. This is illustrated by the Nazi defeat in World War II and the inability of the present Soviet government to produce food sufficient for the population. Totalitarian governments have probably been less effective on the whole than constitutional governments. Pretentious and overbearing, they starkly exemplify what we have noted in so many forms: that it is often the same people who are the masterful and the fated.

We can now examine the situation created by the conflict of man and humanity in somewhat greater detail. We can do this by seeing how we have empowered fate by our responses to each of the demands of destiny as formulated in modern revolutionary ideology—for liberty, equality, and fraternity.

FATE AND LIBERTY

Liberty is glorious because essentially it is being fully oneself and thus being unreservedly human. To enjoy liberty is to draw joy from the depths of personal being, from destiny. But traditional rhetoric so emphasizes the glory of liberty that it obscures its difficulty. This manifests pride, for the difficulty of liberty is owing to perversities and weaknesses in human nature which we gladly ignore. It magnifies fate for it invites us to suppose that we can easily be free, either by simply casting off restraints or by deliberately and quickly creating the conditions of liberty. Since we cannot be free in either of these ways, the result of trying to do so is to lose freedom by acts carried out in pursuit of freedom.

To say that liberty is the state of being unreservedly human is not to minimize—rather, it is to indicate the main reason for—its difficulty. Liberty means living in full consciousness of our finitude and mortality, bound to die yet possessing no rational knowledge of what death means, and responsible in spite of every incertitude and imperfection for choosing and carrying on a life. The glory of liberty consists in inhabiting this situation in a way that gives one's life the form of a destiny. But this cannot be easy or steadily enjoyable. Hence rarely do we wish unreservedly to be free, and when circumstances render it difficult to bear the limits, doubts, and responsibilities of personal life, we prefer not to be free.

There are two principal ways of repudiating liberty. These arise from two ways, already noted, which we have of laying down the burden of our humanity. The first is typified by the despot. At least occasionally, all of us would like to forget our finitude and imperfection and to stand over our lives and history and determine the outcome of events. Some of us occasionally try. The motive is pride and the aim is to be more than human. This means denying the liberty of others. The other way of repudiating liberty is typified by the rank-and-file member of a totalitarian party. All of us occasionally would like to be less than human, to forget our responsibilities and simply live as some exalted power tells us to live. The motive here I have already termed self-abandonment. This too means denying the liberty of others; but here the aim is not to exercise your own despotic liberty but to create a social and political setting in which you can throw away your own liberty, too. In sum, to be free and at the same time fully cognizant of your own limitations and imperfections is onerous. Escape can be sought by denying either the limitations and imperfections or the freedom. There are ominous possibilities of cooperation between those who want to be more and those who want to be less than human—between those who would take liberty from others and those who would be glad to have someone take their liberty.

Hence liberty is possible only within society and under government. Human beings must be voluntarily or forcibly under restraint. Liberties enjoyed must be matched by sacrifices and restrictions, by liberties not enjoyed. Perhaps absolute liberty would be easy if it were possible at all. But liberty within a pattern of responsibilities and restraints is difficult. Intricate institutional arrangements, such as independent courts, are needed, as are social conditions, such as respect for law, without which courts cannot effectively function.

Human beings must also be educated, informed, and encouraged. These things also require institutions—schools, newspapers, forms for comradeship and authority. Here too institutions depend on conditions and attitudes that cannot be deliberately created.

At the same time, the conditions and arrangements on which liberty depends cannot be specified in any final, all-inclusive set of principles. They are infinitely varied and complex. And in their grounds and entirety they are incomprehensible. A society is not even in principle reducible to theoretical propositions. In this way it is like nature or a human being; our theories, using Bergson's characterization, are only snapshots. Hence the near impossibility of a revolution that establishes liberty. Only tentative and piecemeal changes are apt to do that.

Not only does liberty require conditions and arrangements, however; and not only are these beyond final and comprehensive specification. No conditions and arrangements whatever guarantee that liberty will actually come into being. As already noted, between act and aim is an unbridgeable chasm. Public leaders trying to create liberty must sooner or later come to the edge of this chasm. Then they face the mystery of the willingness or unwillingness of people to live in the consciousness of their finitude, mortality, and imperfection, thus rendering themselves accessible to destiny.

Liberty, then, cannot be gained either by casually casting off restrictions or by deliberately willing its conditions. The former ignores the dependence of liberty on conditions, the latter the rational incomprehensibility and necessary inconclusiveness of those conditions. Pride is dangerous to liberty because it obscures these constraints. It encourages indulgence in the notion that people desire freedom unreservedly, both for themselves and for all others, and that freedom therefore is easily achieved. It encourages careless liberation.

It is apparent what the results of careless liberation are apt to be. Despised reality, forgotten amid the imagined glories of absolute and immediate freedom, avenges itself. The fate of those too proud for caution may be nearer to absolute slavery than to absolute liberty. The Soviet state was created by men who were seeking liberty but, imbued with the traditions of Russian autocracy, contemptuous of bourgeois democracy, and inspired by Marxist optimism, knew and cared little about the conditions governing the acquirement of liberty. Unfavorable circumstances, such as the chaos of the Civil War, played a part in the rise of Soviet despotism. But a decisive factor was that the leaders of the Revolution were ignorant and arrogantly neglectful of the social conditions and political arrangements on which liberty depends. The helplessness of Lenin and Trotsky before the machinations of Stalin, for example, is inexplicable apart from their complete unpreparedness—by virtue of temperament, experience, or philosophical orientation—for the task of organizing a loyal opposition.

A similar logic can be seen in the early history of capitalism as well. Capitalism has not been as destructive of liberty as Soviet communism and may even, under some circumstances, be favorable to liberty. In its early years, however, it imposed virtual slavery on the working class and even now, by drawing everyone into a life of thoughtless production and consumption, imperils authentic liberty. Capitalism, like communism, reflects a history of careless liberation. Industrial entrepreneurs, no less brazenly than Bolshevik leaders, laid claim to absolute liberty while knowing and caring little about the conditions of liberty. The oppressive circumstances thus created were the matrix of the Marxist movement.

Observing contemporary capitalism we realize that while liberty depends on supportive social and political institutions, on arrangements that check the human inclination either to deny liberty to others or to refuse liberty for oneself, no institutions or arrangements guarantee anything. Seeing lives devoted to the trivial distractions provided in the capitalist marketplace, to minor comforts and shallow entertainments, we realize that liberty can be lost through developments less dramatic than revolution and political systems less frightening than totalitarian dictatorship.

Also, observing contemporary capitalism, we are reminded that liberty depends finally on a sense of what humanity means. We are reminded that liberty depends on a sense of destiny. Otherwise the requisite patience and strength will be wanting. Separated from a true concept or intuition of humanity, liberty will come either to be looked on as something that purposeful and courageous people should gladly cast aside or else to be equated with merely doing as one pleases, even with the commitment of one's whole life to pleasurable diversions.

There are, then, various forms of careless liberation, some active and some acquiescent, some manifest in deeds of annihilation and some in quiet irresponsibility, some written into terroristic political institutions and some merely implicit in an apparently innocuous interpretation of liberty as personal preference. All in one way or another come from the pride of supposing that liberty can be had simply by willing it, by forgetting that as destiny it requires both receptivity and discipline.

Careless liberation means trying to lay hold of liberty without suffering. The idea that liberty and suffering are connected is remote from modern attitudes. Liberty is supposedly spontaneity and happiness. But consideration of human nature and human circumstances suggests that liberty must mean something more. It must mean care and restraint, acute awareness of finitude and mortality, and perhaps a troubled conscience. If so, there is no liberty without suffering. But suffering cannot be glorious—as liberty presumably is—unless transfigured by destined consequences. This is why liberty that does not resound with destiny is bound to be distorted or rejected.

In the history of liberty, the irony of our fate is that liberation has led to the rise of vast states and organizations which either take liberty by force or else cunningly debase it. It would be misleading to say that since 1789 we have drawn nearer to full liberty but have yet to attain it. We have no doubt in some ways drawn nearer to it. But sometimes, while thinking we were drawing nearer to it, we were actually moving away from it. The kinds of enslavement experienced in recent times cannot be viewed simply as liberty unattained. Enslavement is justified as a requirement of liberty or even as liberty itself. Liberty is often subtly nullified, as in the United States, but in the name of liberty itself. Liberty is forcibly destroyed, but ostensibly in order to force people to be free. To dismiss these justifications as mere rhetoric would be to obscure the ironies of our situation along with the main source of those ironies: that we have tried to lay hold of liberty as though that meant returning, violently or comfortably, to a state of original innocence rather than gaining that demanding and precarious position, both institutional and spiritual, in which we can live according to a vision of what it is given to each one of us to be.

FATE AND EQUALITY

Inequality is one of the most disquieting facts of twentieth century life. This is because it is found practically everywhere—under capitalism, communism, and democratic socialism—and hardly anyone approves of it unreservedly. Those who suffer from inequality burn with resentment and those who profit from it enjoy their privileges with uneasy consciences. Many struggle for privilege and power—but often as outspoken protagonists of equality. The few who defend inequality in principle are compelled by an egalitarian consensus to be qualified and defensive. Judged by prevailing standards, the continuance of inequality is one of the great failures of modern history. The revolutions at the end of the eighteenth century marked the beginning of a great egalitarian movement. Two centuries later, in spite of extensive equalization, the goal seems as unreachable as when the movement began.

This is due partly to the same proud negligence of human limitations that subverted the process of liberation. Total equality is as impossible as total liberty. In nature and accomplishment people are perdurably unequal. They are unequal in vitality, emotional balance, intelligence, physical strength, and in practically every characteristic that can be measured. They also are unequal in art, athletics, scholarship, commerce, and every other activity in which they engage. These irrepressible facts are not nullified by saying that people are *morally* equal—in dignity, in rights, and so forth—although *naturally* unequal, even though such a statement would be true. Natural inequalities cannot be ignored in any sane ordering of society. And not only are people unequal, so are the functions they must perform. To be a cellist demands far greater human resources than to be a barber. To say that both should be equally respected is unconvincing. Superior skill, imagination, and responsibility do, and surely should, call forth commensurate respect.

Moreover, just as the will to freedom is equivocal, so is the will to equality. Very few steadily and undividedly desire an equal apportionment of wealth, power, and privilege. Many would not be content with what they would receive in any such apportionment. Nor would their discontent necessarily be materialistic and selfish; sometimes it would represent a sense of injustice based on valid feelings of personal superiority. Everyone, at times and in ways, resists descending to the level of all others.

To suppose, however, that everyone always and unequivocally desires the superior position would be simplistic. Most of us, at least occasionally and equivocally, are willing for others to stand above us. Motives are various but substantial: relief from responsibility; enjoyment of the spectacle of luxury and rank; satisfaction in feeling that important functions are in able hands.

Careless equalization, consequently, can have results as fateful as careless liberation. Those with unusual energy and ability may refuse to work without unusual rewards; people of ambition and craft may turn a formal system of equality into a facade behind which privileges legally denied are illegally gained and powers ostensibly nonexistent are covertly exercised. Such are the commonplaces of social and political life since 1789.

The ironies of equalization, however, are more sharply etched than those of liberation. Equalization lends itself more readily than does liberation to the intervention of human will. Upper classes can be forcibly deprived of their privileges and powers. Lower classes can deliberately be accorded economic benefits, educational opportunities, and political power. Forcing people to be free is a paradox; forcing them to be equal looks like a plain and indisputable possibility. The ironic reversal of efforts at equalization are therefore unpleasantly surprising. They are also readily comprehensible.

One consequence of deliberately attempting to establish equality is the enthronement of those who lead the attempt. Thus communism nowhere has brought equality but only a shift of powers and privileges to ostensible equalizers. In the constitutional democracies as well, the drive toward equality has brought new dominations and powers: oligarchies commanding egalitarian pressure groups, party leaders elevated through the mechanics of mass participation, governmental bureaucrats enjoying perfect occupational security and complete freedom from popular control.

The will to equality has also aided the rise of the masses, another fateful phenomenon of our times. The masses are not merely the people. They are equalized multitudes, unified and insensitive, standing with giant states and corpora-

tions as one of the brute facts of modern history. Under the
masses the individual finds himself stifled, his destiny ignored
and defeated, not by specific ruling groups but by everyone—everyone fused into a force with a single and omnipresent will. Outwardly, no violation of the principle of
equality occurs. But equality is preserved through uniformity. Hence its spirit is subverted. The idea of equality rests
on the mystery, and consequent incomparability, of persons.
Under the dominion of the masses that idea is subjected to a
fatally literal interpretation and is thus in fact, but not in
form, denied.

The masses have been called into existence partly by
domination and pride. To strive for equality by public policy and political will is almost necessarily to try to make
everyone the same. The effort to plan and control requires
that people be treated on the basis of rational generaliza-
tions—that they be objectified. The effort to plan and control social development in order to achieve equality can
hardly avoid producing, and even seeking, uniformity.
Dealing with human beings objectively and *en masse*, what
can it mean to recognize the equal dignity of everyone
except to treat everyone the same? It is not only the dominant few, the equalizers, who succumb to this logic, however. Uniformity is also willed by the equalized multitudes.
Critics of the masses invariably note their self-assurance—a
pride unlike that of the haughty few, a pride of numbers.
For self-assured masses dissent can seem so exceptional as to
be unnatural and hence unworthy even of being rationally
contested. It is smothered by being scorned or simply
ignored.

Further, that motive so different from but congenial with
pride, the inclination toward self-abandonment, reinforces
the irony of fate here as elsewhere. Doing as everyone does
lightens the burden of selfhood. Repressing dissenters lays to
rest one's own misgivings. In these ways, literal equality fur-
thers the flight from freedom. Often it does this quietly,
within liberal and democratic forms. But not always. Tocqueville and others have noted an affinity between equality

and despotism. In the most powerful despotic states of the twentieth century, both Fascist and Communist, one can discern elements of egalitarianism—egalitarianism that enters into a violent and totalitarian flight from selfhood and freedom.

Here we gain a clear view of the phenomenon already noted in this essay, that of fated government. The task of equalization—economically, socially, educationally—is vast and where it is seriously undertaken necessarily gives rise to governments also vast. Yet these ambitious and gigantic pieces of political machinery cannot accomplish very much because of the ironies that are bound to attend programs of equalization. But if egalitarianism gives rise to large and ineffective governments, it also gives rise to the masses. Hence fated governments face multitudes that are dissatisfied and vocal but not easily reasoned with or managed. Almost every modern government stands ponderous and bewildered before the dilemmas of equality.

The spirit of modern egalitarianism is revealed in the moral relativism that often goes with it. To avoid invidious distinctions, it is denied that good and evil can be objectively distinguished. From the principle that all human beings are equal it is inferred—since human beings embrace various values—that all values are equal. A variation on individual relativism, fitting comfortably with the rule of the masses, is majority relativism. Good is equated with the preference of the greater number, a likely result being the majority despotism that Tocqueville feared in America.

Such views are commercially expedient for they imply that anything is good that people can be induced to buy. They are politically expedient because they eliminate the risky duties of leadership, justifying the comfortable subservience of the politician. They are personally seductive since they do away with the need for moral deliberation and choice. They assure that one will never have to resist or stand apart from the majority.

In these ways destiny is subverted. One who is trying to discover a personal identity in the unfoldment of his life cannot admit that every preference is legitimate. One of the bur-

dens of selfhood is that of having to identify and reject inclinations which, if indulged, would result in the dissipation
of personal being. Egalitarian relativism is akin to liberal
hedonism, which reduces liberty to enjoyment. Both render
easy the conduct of life by saying, in effect, "Live as you
like." Both in this way undermine the disciplines of destiny
and rob us of the very idea of destiny.

Elections in present-day constitutional democracies tell us
a good deal about the limits of modern egalitarianism. The
ideal underlying free elections is political equality, the participation of each person in government. The reality is a
fusion of minority control, mass confusion, and apathy.
Established industrial and political minorities are practically
always able to keep the electoral process from threatening
their power and interests. True, they must gain the tacit or
express approval of the voters (tacit in the case of private
and bureaucratic powers, express in the case of elected officials). They do not do this, however, by engaging them in a
rational process of deliberation on public business. Rather,
trying above all to offend no one, they obscure the alternatives. It can be said that voters get roughly the governments
and policies that they choose. But their choices are narrow
and they are not encouraged to reflect on what they truly
need. The individual voter is demoralized both by the triv-
iality of the issues put forth and by the consciousness that a
solitary vote counts for nothing among the massed votes of
millions. Perhaps governments in this way are held broadly
responsible to the people. But they are not held to the standard of equality—not if that standard expresses a consciousness of the mysterious significance of every human being
(evident in the possession of a destiny). That is not done by
molding millions into a political mass that exercises its fateful
sway through elections.

Ironic inequalities are conspicuous in the aftermath of
revolution. This is because revolution ordinarily means that
human will is uncompromisingly and relentlessly exerted.
The American and French Revolutions assaulted political
inequality but set the stage for the economic inequalities in-

herent in capitalism, inequalities in some ways more drastic than those which the revolutionaries had fought. The Russian Revolution was mounted with the ultimate aim of abolishing these inequalities. What it did instead was establish the despotism of a party bureaucracy. The inequalities now prevailing in the Soviet Union are probably more drastic than those in any of the nations whose revolutionary heritage comes from the eighteenth century.

The ideal of equality is difficult to handle because it is valid but is easily misconstrued. It is valid as an acknowledgement that each person has a destiny and that destinies are incommensurable. It is valid also as a condemnation of domination and of dominant groups. Privileged and powerful classes have a special responsibility for the ascendancy of fate, whether under capitalism or any other system, since even though they themselves are victims of that fate, it is a pleasant fate and is embraced enthusiastically. The situation of the lower classes, however, encourages resistance to fate and perhaps, in some circumstances, receptivity to destiny. But to suppose that overthrowing the upper classes is tantamount to overthrowing fate, and that the lower classes are reliable custodians of human destiny, is to be blind to the universal imperfection of human beings. It is, however subtly or "scientifically," to make scapegoats of the upper classes and gods of the lower classes. Even if classes could be abolished, which is doubtful, fate would not be a mere accident of social structure nor would destiny be within the scope of human will.

Whereas inequality is a fact of nature, equality is a decree of destiny, an imperative stemming from the irreducibility of personality to natural endowments or social roles. The insight that tells us in some particular situation how to subordinate natural inequalities to the requirements of destiny is a gift and not a device of will that can be embodied in a standing policy. It is a gift that depends on our readiness to receive it. Our lack of receptivity explains our strange failure—that even while striking at privilege and rank on one side and abolishing destitution and illiteracy on the other, we have not moved ascertainably closer to equality but find ourselves under new and unforeseen forms of ascendancy. We have been insensitive both to the natural realities that make equality in society and state impossible and to destinies that make it a standard to which we are bound in spite of all natural obstacles to adhere.

Instead of fraternity, we speak today of community. But the meaning is substantially the same, and the ideal of community is as clear a requirement of destiny as are liberty and equality. In the history of moral and political thought the concept of community assumes a confusing variety of forms. Community is seen as a requirement of nature or of God, as ideally parochial or universal, as fundamentally political or ecclesiastical, as organic or monolithic. Sometimes community is envisioned as lost and irrecoverable, sometimes as the *telos* of history. But in one way or another it is again and again asserted that human beings belong together and only together are fully human. The ideal of community has stirred the hope and determination of modern man as powerfully as has the ideal of liberty or equality. It was given its archetypal form by Rousseau shortly before the French Revolution. It has been restated by thinkers of diverse persuasions—communist, socialist, and liberal—and has been pursued by movements that have shaped our history.

The results have been no less discordant with intentions than those gained in the struggle for liberty and equality. Rather than having achieved, or even having approached, communal solidarity such as Rousseau envisioned we feel that we are living in an age of uniquely intense alienation. Judging from fiction, philosophy, and social analysis, in few periods of history have individuals felt as solitary and abandoned as they do today.

The wreckage left by community-building efforts is strewn across the landscape of recent history. (1) In the liberal democracies community has been sought through socialism and programs of pragmatic reform like the New Deal. Conditions prevailing after a generation or more of such efforts have been sharply delineated by radical critics: widespread acquisitiveness; cynicism and rapacity among business corporations; inability on the part of governments to define and act upon reasonable conceptions of the public good; and in the population at large an apathy attributable, in part at least, to a commercially degraded culture. Some of the consequences of reformist community-building have been pointed out also by conservative critics: multitudes demoralized by dependence on welfare benefits; uncontrolled inflation caused at least in part by immense governmental expenditures; a vast bureaucracy unchecked by steady and effective public supervision.

(2) As for radical efforts to raise up communities, these can most succinctly be characterized as tragic. The principal example is Marxist communism. There has been the human grandeur of tragedy—men and women of exceptional gifts prepared to sacrifice physical comfort, social standing, and life for their ideals, for community. There has also been failure on a tragic scale: the death and enslavement of incalculable numbers of human beings, and not as martyrs required for the realization of a new community but as casualties of despotism. Some believe that communism will create real communities in times to come. What is apparent now, however, is that most of the radical protagonists of community became victims or agents of monstrous alienating powers called forth by their own programs and efforts. Communism has outlined in terror the irony of our fate.

(3) Fascism has also had a part in the struggle for community. The history of fascism is not tragic but atrocious. It is the outcome of a desperate effort among alienated men to fuse all things together. This was to be done through national feeling, impassioned leadership, and war. That fascist states have not been communities needs no emphasis. The reasons are not difficult to identify. The fascist concept of community suppresses, as the Communist concept does not,

some of the most distinctive human attributes—intellect, freedom, and a sense of identity with humankind. The reasons for so drastic a distortion of the human image are also apparent. Fascism is a phenomenon of exhausted patience; it is a product of economic, social, and political turmoil. The upshot is a nearly hysterical will to action. Fascist thinkers carry to an irrational extreme the activism of the Western world. A will to action so pressing that no doubt is tolerated inevitably distorts the human image.

These failures, of course, are shaped by conditions peculiar to the nations and times in which they occurred. Beyond the particularities of place and period, however, there is a more general circumstance that has obstructed the modern movement toward community and, more than this, has been the primary source of modern alienation. This is industrialism, with conditions such as the mobility, specialization, standardization, and hierarchical organization to which it has given rise. We must look toward industrialism for an explanation of the fact that two centuries after the time of Rousseau the alienation that made Rousseau an exceptional and haunting figure, and impelled him to formulate his communal ideal, is now the fate of almost everyone.

On the one hand, industrialism inevitably creates conditions that are hostile to community. These are the result of subjecting human beings to precise and extensive rational organization and are exemplified by the equation of every person with a function and by the ascendancy of a managerial elite. Some conditions of this kind no doubt can be subordinated to communal purposes and relationships. But in assuming that all of them can, and that industrialism and community are fully harmonious, communists and socialists have been guilty of a proud carelessness like that which we have noted in the modern pursuit of liberty and equality.

On the other hand, industrialism creates opportunities, as well as obstacles, for community. The opportunities are mainly those inherent in material plenty. Community depends on serious communication, hence on the search for truth, hence on leisure. Until the industrial revolution this chain of presuppositions was anchored in one final presupposition, devastating for community: slavery, or some variation thereof. Leisure, and true communal activity, were possible only for those freed from labor by the enforced labor of others. This was one source of the tragedy of Hellenic civilization. Beneath the brilliance of Periclean Athens lay the darkness of slavery and empire. By providing machines to take the place of slaves, industrialism eliminated this final presupposition and thus removed one of the largest and oldest obstacles to community.

Strangely, however, it seems likely that the opportunities, as well as the obstacles, have contributed to modern alienation. This is because of the particular coloring they have given to modern pride. It is easy to see that industrialism reinforces pride and that pride is unfavorable to community. People in industrial societies naturally survey their inventions and their factories and assume that these prove their sovereignty. And confident of their sovereignty they are insensitive to the unfathomable and uncontrollable realities that go into the making of community. Fully to understand these attitudes, however, it is necessary to realize how they have been affected by the possibilities for community which we see before us.

These possibilities render the obstacles to community exasperating, if not intolerable. Industrialism creates unprecedented opportunities for community at the same time that it raises up obstacles that are not only novel but are peculiarly obstinate, since they are inherent in the very processes that bring about material plenty and obviate the necessity of class divisions. Thus industrialism opens up prospects which it simultaneously closes off. It denies the hope it arouses. The resultant tension is what gives the writings of Marx much of their vitality. Capitalism is analyzed in terms of the paradox of historical possibilities at once established and foreclosed. The release of the tension set up by this paradox is at the source of the revolutionary spirit of Marx and his followers. The opposition between community and industrial order is reduced to the opposition of proletariat and bourgeoisie, and this, given the productivity of an industrial economy, is readily held to be temporary. We can see in Marxism, however, not only recognition of the tension resulting from hope simultaneously affirmed and denied. We also can see exemplified the effects of this tension on the pride of industrial man.

The contradiction between communal possibilities and alienating realities is a peculiarly restless and exasperated pride. This is manifest in the revolutionary temper of Marx and his followers and in their reluctance to take into account the alienating conditions inherent in industrial organization. It is evident in their neglect of the likelihood that these conditions would be perpetuated not only by the imperatives of industrialism but also by human nature, by an enduring will to power and to wealth. But such impatience is not found among Marxists alone. All modern political movements—liberalism, communism, fascism, even conservatism—have been infused with the idea that it is possible to create community by action. Thus industrialism, beyond heightening the pride natural to all of us and present in all historical periods, has, by making community so exasperatingly near yet distant, given this pride an urgency that is historically unique.

Heightening and exacerbating pride, industrialism also has increased the blindness that goes with pride. Modern communal hopes have reflected a neglect not only of anticommunal necessities inherent in industrial organization but also of powerful inclinations among human beings to ally themselves with these necessities. Industrial organization serves both pride and despair. It offers historically unprecedented possibilities of ascendancy (as through advanced weaponry and propaganda spread by means of the mass media) and of self-abandonment (as through organizational routine and televised entertainment). The soaring hopes expressed in modern political movements attest our readiness to overlook our own weaknesses. How neglectful, for example, has modern political idealism in its Marxist and liberal forms alike been of the human characteristics that make totalitarianism, with the profound alienation created by terror and one-party propaganda, a possibility at even the highest stages of industrial development.

Of particular interest in connection with "fraternity," however, is the blindness of people in industrial societies to the only pathway to that end, to community—that is, communication. Community is brought into being through speaking and listening and in no other way. It is found in shared truth. Communication is precluded, however, when human beings are approached altogether as objects of action. Hence the pride of thinking that community could be created by action—a pride colored with impatience and anger by the ambiguity of industrialism, beautiful in its promise and desolating in its reality—has been worse than a source of difficulties. It has assured that communal efforts would be self-defeating. People of the Western world have had such success in technology and engineering that they can ponder their ideals only as problems of action. Conceiving of community in this fashion, they have not had the patience for communication, a task requiring willingness to wait and to abide uncertain results.

One consequence of the impatient demand for community without communication has been the proliferation of ideologies. An ideology is a set of ideas designed to mobilize the masses for the attainment of immediate unity. An ideology is both a purported explanation of historical forces and a program of action. It claims complete and absolute truth and hence demands total commitment. An ideology is worldly, tacitly or explicitly repudiating "pie in the sky" and calling for unity here and now. Although human beings have an inherent yearning for the sense given them by ideologies, that all is known and the future assured, industrialism may intensify this yearning. Ideologies rest on the premise, made plausible by industrialism, that people can act on their whole situation with an understanding as complete and confident as that with which they act on physical objects. And ideologies ordinarily respond to the hopes aroused by industrialism. They magnify the communal possibilities, and minimize or deny the alienating imperatives, established by industrialism. It would not be far wrong to define ideologies as systems of popular thought promising to resolve the paradox that community is near at hand but unreachable.

Ideologies inspire indoctrination and stifle the patience and openness required for communication. Socialism, communism, and fascism have all crystallized as ideologies, and have borne the crucial ideological mark, a passion for community accompanied by hostility to communication. In making community an object of action, while discouraging communication, ideologies logically gives rise to politics centered on the arts of propaganda.

An emphatic sign of the impact on community of activist impatience is that the very media of "communication" have taken on fated qualities and stand between man and being, massive and opaque, cultivating superficiality and smothering reason. Television, radio, and the press are for the most part media of advertising and entertainment, not of communication in any serious sense. Our very willingness to speak of them as media of communication suggests a certain communal insensibility.

The modern quest for community comes to a climax in a phenomenon that is as near to being an organized and total denial of community as any social entity with the coherence necessary to survive in history could be—the totalitarian state. Both communist and fascist totalitarianism are products of impassioned efforts to establish community here and now. Both in fact force on everyone in their power extreme alienation, the very condition of their massive unity being the terrified silence and solitude in which every citizen lives.

The modern struggle for community, like that for liberty and equality, has been abortive because it has been carried on without humility, without awareness that common discovery of truth, in which serious communication and hence authentic community consists, is not under anyone's command. Hence action aiming at community must stop short of the goal; it can create conditions favoring community, but not community itself. Action arising from pride and carried forward with impatience, action unwilling to recognize the necessity of stopping short, is bound to have ironical results—forms of unity, like the totalitarian state, that may be communal in name but are anticommunal in reality.

The concern for community is in itself closely allied with the concern for destiny. Only through communication do we enter the interpersonal sphere of being where destinies are discovered and lived. "So long as the heaven of *Thou* is spread out over me," a great philosopher of community has written, "the winds of causality cower at my heels, and the whirlpool of fate stays its course."[1] But "the heaven of Thou" cannot be designed and constructed as can a factory. Some things belong to hope.

FATE AND TRUTH

Liberty, equality, and fraternity all are requirements of destiny. They express a consciousness of the mystery of a human being, of an entity who cannot be comprised in any social or political definition, and must therefore be given room to exist beyond all customary and legal roles—liberty; must be granted a respect not measured by the standards of any social or political hierarchy—equality; and is homeless and incomplete except in a state of deep and unforced unity with others of his kind—fraternity. When we have formulated our sense of destiny in these ideals, we must live by them and that means we must try to bring about a reformation of society and state. Destiny otherwise would be drowned in hypocrisy. But destiny is also lost if we decide that the reformation of society and state must occur according to human will and design—if we strive for reformation without receptivity. In that case we can realize our ideals only in degraded forms—liberty as mere unconstraint, equality as uniformity, community as totalitarian unity. Will produces caricatures of the demands of destiny.

Probably none of our ideals or standards has escaped this

fateful inversion. It might be possible to analyze the modern mind in detail, showing the ironic transformations undergone by such standards as sincerity, happiness, and fidelity. One ideal seems particularly worthy of attention, however, and that is truth.

Truth is the presence of being in consciousness and the bond among persons. It is the substance of mind and community. Destiny is the order of personal being. As the Logos, it is the order of all being. Hence destiny is found only in the truth. In community, we seek and share the truth which is known and lived as destiny. In our relationships with truth our destiny is decided. What has happened to these relationships?

In a way, they are flourishing. Never in history has so much been known nor have so many had access to what is known. Awesome progress in the physical sciences, the refinement and exploitation of techniques for gathering and analyzing data in the social sciences, the development of mass circulation newspapers and magazines and of continental radio and television networks, and the opening up of university education to all who are interested: in these and other ways the ordinary individual in a modern Western nation has access to an amount of information which can place him in a world far more carefully observed and available for inspection than the world of the most alert and educated mind of any preceding age.

When speaking of this situation, however, we ordinarily use words like "information" and hesitate to say that what we know is "truth." Afloat on a sea of facts, nowhere on the horizon do we see the truth as a stable and integral reality. In the midst of unprecedented accumulations of knowledge we possess no unified vision and feel no assurance as to what is important and what is trivial. This applies to various fields. For all of the progress in the physical sciences, the average person does not have even a sketchy understanding of the overall nature of the physical universe; in public affairs we are overwhelmed with information but do not know what is really happening to us; so far as ultimate realities are concerned—realities of the kind traditionally sought by philosophers and theologians—educated people (including many professors of philosophy and religion) take refuge in a staunch and sophisticated agnosticism. For all of our riches, we are distressingly impoverished. In a sense, knowing almost everything, in actuality we know nothing.

Our plight is starkly manifest in American universities. Ostensibly dedicated to the discovery and sharing of the truth, in fact even at their best they are loose groupings of scholars cultivating small and tenuously related fields of knowledge. More commonly, they are organizations made up of people with high academic credentials but indifferent to research, preoccupied with the organizational problems of their institutions, and providing their students with little more than gilded vocational training.

Our poverty of understanding is visible also in government. Present-day officials command information so extensive that in comparison the knowledge possessed by most earlier governments looks like mere ignorance. Yet seldom can leaders cogently define the principal issues facing their governments, and the best journalists are merely accurate regarding facts and skilled in conjecture. The public is divided between multitudes who are ignorant and indifferent (but neither stupid nor invariably wrong in their political judgments) and a few who are well-informed but confused. Occasionally, as during the American war in Vietnam, it is said that the average citizen lacks the information needed for judging public issues. In the liberal democracies that is rarely true. Far more information is available than the average citizen can review. The problem is in grasping and using it.

The vast sums of knowledge at our disposal, however, are not simply riches we are unable at the moment to spend. They are used to our detriment and in this way, like our physical wealth, constitute a fate. They are used for multiplying commercially profitable products that often bring no more than pleasure and diversion and sometimes bring disease and death. They guide the building of weapons sys-

tems able to destroy civilizations. Our capacities for gathering
and storing information about people is such that we reasonably fear the systematic destruction of personal privacy.
Medical technology can keep people alive and functioning
for years after they would have died in earlier times but it
also places before everyone the prospect of a prolonged and
ruinously expensive death.

Just as we do not know what all of our knowledge means,
neither do we have much idea of its purpose. No wonder it
has been misused. Its magnitude, and our inability to discern its meaning and proper ends, invites heedless and selfish
exploitation. Again we see it as fate—massive, threatening,
and in its totality incomprehensible. In some ways it provides
us with as enigmatic and ominous a circumambience as did
the unknown natural universe for primitive man.

What we lack is truth as a disclosure of our destinies and
of environing reality as a setting for the enactment of destinies. Truth has traditionally been revered because of the
faith that human beings belonged in the universe and that
the unfoldment of their humanity would take place as they
found their way into the heart of being. There was a corre-
spondence between man and being; in discovering the truth
people found the outlines of their destinies written in the
realities around them.

Someone may say in our defense that we have simply cast
aside the illusions and fancies of earlier times. That is a legitimate matter for discussion. But we would flatter ourselves if
we thought that only a resolute pursuit of the truth has
brought us to our present situation. It is not truth as such
that modern man has sought but truth of a particular kind:
truth that is verifiable and usable. We have wanted truth that
we could hold securely in our possession, demonstrate in
order to silence doubters, and use to bring the world around
us under control. In other words, it has been the will to
mastery that has motivated the modern pursuit of truth.
Often in the past human beings felt humbled by the truth.
They felt that they had to await its disclosure and might live
in its presence but never possess it; that they could not by

rational argumentation compel the uncertain or disputatious to acknowledge it; and that they could not employ the truth for power and profit but had to let the truth, as it were, employ them. They sometimes found, like Socrates, that being employed by the truth was a sacrificial calling. Today many assume that truth of this kind does not exist. But whether it exists or not, modern man has not tried to find it, for he has not wanted a humbling truth.

The pursuit of truth thus was fateful for the same reasons that the pursuit of liberty, equality, and fraternity was fateful. It was carried on blindly, without regard for realities, such as man and transcendence, that could not in their nature be included in the kind of truth that was sought. It was carried on without regard for the dangers inherent in possessing knowledge that could be drastically consequential in our physical lives yet was gained by neglecting wisdom.

The fatefulness of truth of the kind we have cherished and learned can be seen in its effects on community. Established factual knowledge is not a bond of community if community comes into being through communication and communication is common inquiry. Anyone disputing factual knowledge must simply be refuted or ignored, and the process of refutation is one-sided and coercive. Moreover, knowledge that can be rationally established is necessarily incomplete. Some questions, such as those concerning God and value, cannot be unequivocally and demonstrably answered. But these are the questions that matter above all others. They bear on things which as matters of mutual agreement or common inquiry lie at the foundations of community. People united in established knowledge alone are united superficially. Hence pursuing factual knowledge as though it were truth itself has necessarily been destructive of community. This is exemplified in the cultural and personal alienation that is apt to be suffered by anyone today in America who, in the conduct of serious inquiry, ignores academic boundaries, commercial utility, and social fashions.

The extreme of modern epistemological pride is reached in the practice, common in totalitarian nations, of deliberately manufacturing the truth. Explanations of biological evolution and accounts of recent history have both been consciously fashioned in order to conform with ideology and serve state power. As the modern quest for community comes to a climax in the totalitarian state, the age of science culminates in societies in which science, history, and philosophy are products of official decree.

Glancing back over the terrain we have crossed in the last two chapters, it is apparent that fate assumes a variety of forms—a defiled earth, stultifying work, alien wealth; also governments that are large and ineffective, masses politically uninformed but demanding, knowledge vast in extent and power but humanly insignificant and therefore threatening. Fundamentally, however, fate is a characteristic of time, as is destiny. Hence it is a form taken by history. To see it in this way will be our aim in the following chapter.

5

THE FURY OF HISTORY

DESTINY, TIME, AND HISTORY

LET US PAUSE AND renew our grip on the central idea of this essay, that of destiny. To do that can help us to keep in view the overall theme of these reflections in spite of the numerous complexities in which we necessarily become involved. It can help us also to see clearly why in discussing fate and destiny we must necessarily consider time and therefore history. Recurring to the central concept of the inquiry can make it plain why at some point we would have to face some of the perplexities of that most perplexing of subjects, the philosophy of history.

The concept of destiny is a response to the sense of personal contingency, the powerful and disquieting impression that one's existence is merely accidental. The sense of personal contingency is both ontological and moral. As ontological, it is essentially a feeling of vulnerability. Originating accidentally, one feels at every moment of life wholly exposed to circumstances. Each person, as Marcus Aurelius wrote, inhabits an unfortified city. Circumstances may, slowly or suddenly, and in either case inexplicably and irresistibly, rearrange or abolish one's existence. In its moral aspect, the sense of contingency is that life is without purpose or justification. Sartre expressed this impression when he spoke of man as "a useless passion." The universe is neither informed with teleological order nor upheld by divine love.

The sense of contingency provokes a rebellion against

time. Contingency is a temporal state. To feel that one's existence is wholly accidental—ontologically vulnerable and morally meaningless—is to experience the anguish of time. It is therefore natural for human beings to condemn time and to look for ways of rising above it. Our major activities are often shaped by this motive.

Thus the ideal of complete and perfect knowledge, in secure human possession, is an ideal of supra-temporal existence. Scientific research is a contest with time and rests on the premise that reason can conduct us into a sphere of unconditionality. This is a strategy of contemplation and in its historical origins is Hellenic. We also strive for superiority to time through the moral law—through attempting to frame and perfectly obey eternally valid rules of conduct. This strategy is activist rather than contemplative, and is Hebraic in its historical origins. In art we attempt to create masterpieces which will never go out of fashion and never be forgotten. In politics we try to form states invulnerable to decay. Every ideology, affirming an invariable pattern of history or an unconditional ideal of political order, is in one way or another an assault on time.

Defiance of temporality, however, involves willful blindness to our ontological state and is the quintessence of pride. In mythical Christian terms, the deep and persisting inclination to engage in such defiance is "original sin." Both the Hellenic quest for redemption through knowledge and the Hebraic effort to win justification through perfect obedience to the law are patterned after Adam's mythic sin. They are aimed at definitive knowledge of good and evil. In this way they constitute a refusal of human limitations. Man is essentially finite and thus immanent. The attempt to rise into a state of changeless truth, goodness, beauty, or order depends on intentional obliviousness of our ontological condition. "Behold," God says on casting Adam out of the Garden of Eden, "the man has become like one of us, knowing good and evil."[1] The result, as we have seen in preceding chapters, is the ascendancy of time in its most frightening and destructive form, that of fate. Here we see a dialectic of moral experience in which we are forcibly confronted with our temporality.

Many will here feel at a standstill. If we cannot rise above time, it will be presumed that contingency is inescapable. There is an ancient tradition in the West that sets time and reality in irreconcilable opposition to one another. The real is supratemporal and time is an invasion of nothingness. This tradition is represented in Plato's doctrine of forms and in Gnostic dualism. To the extent that we are affected by this tradition we will feel that if we are condemned to temporality then we are condemned altogether. Our lives and being are thoroughly and irremediably contingent.

There is another tradition in Western thought and faith, however. Time and reality, according to this tradition, are mysteriously in accord. Not only can time be a disclosure of reality; the accord is so basic that reality is not disclosed except in time. This view was established in Western thought by the Old Testament. Time in the form of the history of Israel was the revelation of God to his people, and God did not reveal himself in any other way. The most concentrated and dramatic representation of the oneness of time and reality is the Christian doctrine of the Incarnation: in Jesus the temporal and eternal become one being. It is not only in biblical theology, however, that this tradition is reflected. In the philosophy of Kant, for example, a moral act is a kind of incarnation. As moral, it is a manifestation of eternal imperatives; as an act, it is temporal. It cannot be said that such an act is *partly* supratemporal and *partly* temporal. The unity of time and eternity is as complete and as rationally inexplicable in Kantian moral theory as in Christian theology.

The idea of destiny is derived from the second of these traditions. To help in defining destiny we can distinguish three main principles in the second tradition. (1) A human being can be redeemed from contingency without being raised above time; paradoxically, unconditionality and temporality are compatible. (2) *Human* unconditionality is attained, however, only through *divine* unconditionality, through God's mercy; and God, unlike man, transcends time even though He enters into time. (3) Human unconditionality is attained *only* in time. For Jews and Christians salvation does not come as it does for Plato, through suprahistorical wisdom, but only through entering fully into history and time; God is encountered here and now. Thus we are brought back to the definition of destiny given in chapter 2: unconditioned selfhood, given by transcendence, and realized in time.

It would be extremely misleading were the impression to be created that destiny is rationally understandable. In dividing reality and time Plato was unquestionably following the requirements of reason. How that which is wasted by time can be fully real, how the temporal and the unconditional can be joined, how one being can be both historical and eternal (these questions are ultimately the same) cannot be explained. The idea of destiny can be defended only as a matter of faith and personal experience. In this sense it rests on grounds some may regard as weak. They are no weaker, however, than those underlying the biblical concept of history, the Christian doctrine of the Incarnation, and the Kantian principle that moral acts enter into the temporal order of phenomenal events.

Whatever the grounds of the concept of destiny, however, the consequences are clear. We must accept our temporality. We must live in time in order to be accessible to our destinies. Destiny is a form of time, transfigured time. Defiance of time is therefore not merely a refusal to accept our ontological condition; it is unreceptive to destiny. Openness toward transcendence is not a yearning to be relieved of temporality. It is possible only for one who is able lucidly and responsibly to inhabit time. To be receptive to one's destiny is to be alert to intimations of meaning in time.

One is not concerned merely with personal time, however. If destiny is universally human and not exclusively personal, then one is concerned with time in its most comprehensive form and that is history. One is open toward transcendence and receptive to destiny by living as a historical being.

Efforts to discern meaning in history therefore are proper to all of us. If destiny is deliverance from contingency, then all circumstances without exception serve the unfoldment of the self. "All things," as Paul said, "work together for good to them that love God, to them who are the called according to his purpose."[2] World history comprises all things and should contain intimations of meaning if destiny is real. Thus the philosophy of history arose from the biblical revelation of destiny, and Augustine, facing the apparent historical absurdity of the fall of Rome, felt called upon to show that history was not in truth absurd but that, for those accepting the destiny made available to man through Christ, "all things worked together for good."

This brings us to a crucial principle, that of historical continuity. If time falls to pieces, so that events and periods are not related comprehensibly, then one cannot live in time. One must then orient oneself toward a particular segment of time, such as an idealized period of the past or the pleasures offered by the present moment. Nor can one find meaning in history. Discontinuity is manifest meaninglessness. This is not to imply that destiny is realized as a story that can be embodied in an objective account. Rather, it is an incommunicable personal experience. Hence an individual's destiny cannot be made plain in a biography, nor can human destiny be shown in a pattern of historical events. The greatest biographies may, like James Boswell's *Life of Johnson*, pay little attention to the order of facts displayed by a life, and the greatest philosophies of history may, like Augustine's, make little sense of the order of events. Destiny is experienced in a mysterious sense of significance often evoked by such works. But no such sense of significance can be evoked where continuity is manifestly lacking. Destiny is denied by the sound and fury of events. Without continuity, a personal life must seem to be that of an idiot and history to be nothing more than a series of accidents.

Historical continuity is therefore an elemental need. This pertains to our situation today.

Fateful history is broken history. We do not experience fate in the form of a vast story, comprising all past and future ages, and leading irresistibly to a final catastrophe. Rather, we are unable to connect events with one another. This may happen in a variety of ways, but in its most comprehensive form it means that we are unable to connect the past and the future in an enduring present. Each stands as a fate in itself. As the idea of destiny implies, one lives out of the past and into the future and has one's being in the present that is thus created. And since each person is a communal being, whose destiny is universally human, the temporal continuum in which one lives must be historical and not merely personal. Hence the loss of historical continuity does not merely deprive us of something we value but can live without. It jeopardizes our humanity.

We are alienated from the past so deeply that recent generations seem separated from us by thousands of years. Merely a century ago people heard of events only days and weeks after their occurrence, traveled rarely and slowly, and, most of them, tilled the soil. Men and women still living were born into a world that knew little of Marx and nothing of Freud, was unacquainted with bolshevism and fascism, and in its most hopeless moments had never imagined anything like the Battle of Verdun or the death camp at Auschwitz. In no century but ours has there been nuclear fission or space exploration, movies or television. We can scarcely imagine how it felt to live just a hundred years ago.

Yet we are not wholly severed from the past. On the contrary, we have been formed by it and it enters into our being in more ways than we can understand and control. Americans for whom Puritan villages and frontier ranches have a legendary distance and charm may carry on their jobs with a grim zeal inherited from Puritan villagers or support a foreign policy conceived according to an ethos of proud and competent violence handed down from frontier ranchers. Times change, and with them attitudes. But attitudes change more slowly than circumstances, and we cannot objectify and master our attitudes as well as we can our circumstances. In this sense we cannot disentangle ourselves from the past.

While the past is strange, then, it continually intrudes in the present, and it does so in ways that are threatening to us. What we have been is not necessarily what we should be now, or even what we should have been in the past. The Puritan work ethic and frontier individualism may not be appropriate for all, or even for any, times and places. But since they enter into the very structure of our minds, we cannot stand off from them and appraise them as we might articles offered for sale.

The past is thus a fate—something alien and dangerous which we cannot wholly understand or control or evade. It is no use trying to meet this situation by looking back nostalgically and glorifying the institutions and ways of our forefathers. Some do this. The past in its essence, they say, is not a fate but rather defines our very humanity. Any wisdom or virtue we possess is an inheritance. Hence we should guard the past and dwell within it, according to this counsel. To condemn the past, as radicals typically do, is to condemn what is best in ourselves. Thus the savagery of revolutions. We are told, in other words, that the past which seems so alien and inhospitable is in truth our only home.

The idea of bridging the chasms that divide us from the past, of becoming consciously and fully what we have been and are condemned in some measure to continue being, must appeal to all of us. It is a project of healing time, thus healing ourselves. It does not take account, however, of how irreparably we have broken the continuity of history. The strangeness of the past may be the work of a delusory pride, but it is not itself a delusion. The past intrudes into the present, but as fate and not as unrecognized destiny. It can be turned into destiny only by being subordinated to the future. We cannot efface the results of the economic, intellectual, and political revolutions of recent times.

And even if we could, is it clear that we should? The past that Edmund Burke evokes in his *Reflections on the French Revolution* is a mansion of traditions and memories, filled with treasures of wisdom. Such a vision may provide grounds for resisting revolutionary pride, but it does this by appealing to pride of another kind—pride in what we have already done. It is true that we are what we have been, but one thing this means is that we are guilty; the past is not a record of virtue triumphant. The celebrants of the past sometimes claim to be more Christian than their revolutionary opponents. But authentic Christians, like revolutionaries, hold that we must look back with regret and remorse. They see human beings as fitted for a life other than the life provided by established societies and they must therefore defend, if not exercise, a paradisiacal imagination. Surely it is the Christians and revolutionaries who are right. In what past can Americans find themselves as they wish to be? In an age when slaves were owned and marketed? When Indians were coolly cheated and wantonly slaughtered? In the decades of the industrial robber barons? In the time of Hiroshima and Nagasaki? Not that all of our deeds have been shameful, but in no past undistorted by sentimentality do we find ourselves in our full humanity. Conservatives argue that ancient institutions, shaped over a long span of time, contain the wisdom and righteousness of many generations. How can they ignore the fact that such institutions are also repositories of folly and selfishness?

This is to say nothing of the claims of the future. Even if the past were all that some of Burke's most glowing passages suggest, would all duties be fulfilled by living within and guarding its changeless forms? Could that be destiny? Not, surely, for a being gifted with the power of criticism and innovation. As shallow as it is to think that the new is always better, it is equally shallow to think that a destiny can be experienced without experiencing the new and facing its uncertainties.

The past follows us like a strange and accusing shadow—something we can neither identify ourselves with nor leave behind. The future, it might be assumed, is very different. Surprisingly, however, it is broadly the same. It, too, is strange and inconceivable. The scientific discoveries, technological developments, intellectual revolutions, and social and political transformations which almost certainly lie ahead cover the future with a darkness as impenetrable as that which enshrouds the past. Most generations have been able to assume that life in the future would be much as it is in the present. Today, however, we must read science fiction in order to imagine how our descendants will live.

The future, like the past, is dangerous. Indeed, there may be no future. But a nuclear holocaust is only the most dramatic of the possibilities that sober calculation must acknowledge. Barbarism is perhaps more likely in view of much in popular culture. A stultifying militarism (a kind of barbarism, perhaps) is prefigured by the bitter relationships of nations that are poor and rich, Islamic and secular, communist and capitalist. Biological degeneration is a possibility suggested by the uncomprehended changes we are effecting in food, water, air, and other elements of the life-supporting environment.

The future is fated, finally, in its inevitability. Like the past, it forces itself upon us. We feel ourselves inexorably propelled out of the present. We continue to investigate and criticize; to invent, produce, and sell; to experiment, discard, and revise. Such activities are pursued as though preordained. We could not moderate them if we wished to, and if we wished to moderate them, and could, our consciences would condemn us. The result, a sum of consequences largely unforeseen, is a future that comes upon us as swiftly and irresistibly, and sometimes as disastrously, as a tidal wave.

In this situation, resolutely pressing ahead, as though the forbidding appearance of the future is sure to disappear on closer acquaintance, is as futile as withdrawing into the past.

There are celebrants of the future, as there are of the past. Both look on man as a being who creates himself. Those who urge us into the future, however, believe that the decisive act of self-creation has yet to occur. Human beings as they now exist offer only glimmerings, or an occasional example, of what humanity can be. By dedicating ourselves to the future we identify ourselves with what we really are. Che Guevara spoke with this voice when he said that as revolutionaries men and women reach the highest level of the human species.[3]

Our links with the past, however, are not merely links of sentiment that we can break if we decide that we should. They are links forged by our finitude—a finitude which prevents us from completely transcending what we are and have been. The similarities of the *ancien régime* and revolutionary France, and of Soviet and Czarist Russia, have been often noted. They reflect the major irony of revolutionary experience, the reappearance of the repudiated past. Since human beings cannot in their finitude transform themselves, they are subject to an imperative of historical continuity. When this imperative is not complied with willingly, it is executed fatefully, in ironic contravention of human intent.

Even if we could liberate ourselves from the past, moreover, we could not necessarily leave behind our imperfections. Celebrants of the future foresee not only a new, but an innocent, humanity. Such a vision naturally appeals to us but there is little in human experience to justify it.

In summary, our alienation from the past and the future is profound. It is not to be overcome by resolutely turning in one direction or the other. We are essentially finite and temporal, and we necessarily have both a past and a future. To concentrate exclusively on one is to turn our backs to the other and by arrogantly ignoring it further empower it as fate. And it is not as though we master that segment of history on which we concentrate. That is neither within our ontological or moral capacities. Ever since late in the eighteenth century people in the West have engaged with unusual intensity in a competitive glorification of past and future. This fact testifies to an increased willingness to ignore the ontological limitations and moral imperfections of humanity. And rather than restoring historical continuity it is a major sign of its loss.

Alienated from the past and future, we are crowded into a narrow and evanescent present—a moment that is only a temporal fragment, vanishing so quickly it is almost nothing. The dazzled preoccupation with the here and now which is so characteristic of contemporary life is evidence less of a happy facility for shedding care than of our fate.

We are told, of course, that the moment is all that we can ever have and that we should therefore live for it. This is a message implicit in much entertainment and advertising and it is given philosophical form in the doctrine of hedonism. But trying to grasp being and selfhood in the present, while ignoring the past and the future, is like trying to grasp a handful of water; it is gone the instant one takes hold. We not only *have* a past and future, we *are* our past and future. To be confined to the present moment, therefore, is to be alienated from oneself and in that sense to be nothing.

The only genuine and realizable present is one in which the past and future are focused and harmonized. It is a space in which the past and future, rather than being excluded, as when the present is conceived of as a chronological segment of time, meet in the temporal experience of a receptive human being. A real present presupposes continuity. The fragmentation of time, alienating us from the past and future, alienates us from the real present as well.

The source of continuity, and thus of an inhabitable present, is a sense of destiny. To live a destiny is to find one's true being in time. It is to live in a present that reconciles the past and future by giving them significance in a personal life. In other words, selfhood is discovered in an experience of significant (destined) continuity.

This experience, at first purely personal (at least in our individualistic culture), becomes historical when one realizes the historical character of one's being: that one is part of all humanity in one's interests and allegiance, and that one is formed by the distant past and dependent for the meaning of one's existence on the distant future. A sense of personal destiny can be enlarged in this way into a sense of the meaning of history. The consciousness of temporal continuity in one's own life helps to heal historical time.

To say that our history today is a fate is to say that we see nothing of ourselves, as we authentically are, in the course of events. We have given up even the idea that we might. Defining ourselves as rational will, we have abandoned receptivity and have approached history with ambitions of mastery. But failing in mastery, and divested on our own initiative of our destiny, we stand as strangers before historical processes we have disrupted and cannot comprehend.

We find ourselves, then, in a cul-de-sac. Worse, there is little disposition to retrace our steps. The two principal political doctrines addressed to us in this situation both are affirmations of human will.

WILL AND HISTORY

Liberalism embodies elements inherited from Greece, Rome, and the Middle Ages. It is an amalgam of many metals, some of them highly precious. There is truth, nevertheless, in Harold Laski's characterization of liberalism as "the philosophy of a business civilization."[4] It was formed by this fact more than by any other phase of its history. It became a doctrine of the power of will. It was the philosophy of the industrial bourgeoisie, the group which more than any other concentrated in itself the willfulness of modern man. And it has been the outlook of those, prior to the twentieth century, who led in the attempted conquest of the physical universe—financiers, political leaders, engineers, and scientists. Reformulated as a defense of collective reform, such as that carried out by the New Deal, liberalism still tells us how people should act in order to impose their purposes on history. The faults commonly attributed to liberalism, such as hedonism, relativism, and acquisitiveness, all are necessary or accidental results of its underlying willfulness. And even the individualism which is at the core of liberalism, and attacked above all else by most critics of liberalism, is objectionable primarily because it is a willful individualism. It does not say to the individual, "Enter uncompromisingly with your own truth into the human community," but rather, "Have your own way, and do not concern yourself with the human community."

The latter was welcome advice for the generations that first became cognizant of the powers and opportunities created by industrialism. Liberalism quickened a multitude of separate wills and incurred the disability repeatedly attacked by Marxists and others: liberal regimes have great difficulty in defining and furthering the common good. Capitalism exhibits the willful individualism sanctioned by liberalism, and classical economics, the doctrine on which capitalism rests, is primarily an effort to show that the common good emerges naturally—without being defined and pursued through politics—from the conflict of individual wills.

In emancipating individual will liberalism is necessarily fateful. Not only does it, by exalting will, induce vulnerability to the irony of fate, but it also, by fragmenting will, leaves the outcome of events to unforeseeable and unmanageable concatenations of individual acts. Even when the common good is attained through following liberal prescriptions, it is less a human achievement than an accident of fate. That we can rely upon such accidents is the main contention of classical economics.

Class conflict, as Marxism charges, necessarily enters into liberal fate. Only a few can respond successfully to the liberal call to action (here too, as everyone knows, much that is accidental is involved) and the ascendancy they gain over nature is bound to be at the same time an ascendancy over human beings. The relationships thus established inevitably become embodied in more or less stable ways of life and thought—in classes.

Reformist liberalism stems from a consciousness of these weaknesses, but it is doubtful whether it really overcomes them. Rarely do we gain from liberal writers, even from the most sophisticated of them, the sense that human beings are under any obligation beyond that of fulfilling their wants and needs in as intelligent and harmless a fashion as possible. Marxists ordinarily express a stronger sense of destiny than do liberals, although their doctrine contains no formal recognition of destiny. By its individualistic willfulness liberalism is betrayed into a fundamental aimlessness. This is the reason why liberal regimes, although reformist in intent, are seldom able to provide a compelling vision of the common good.

Marxism is clearly the most cogent and influential alternative to liberalism. The fatefulness of liberalism, it might be said, is the center of the Marxist attack. This attack grows out of an effort to solve the puzzle of modern history: as our technological and industrial powers unfold, we increasingly become playthings of historical forces that we cannot comprehend. The augmentation of human power seems to have been accompanied by a lessening of historical control. In short, the main problem for Marxist thought is the fatefulness of history. The explanation is found in liberalism as an economic system, that is, in capitalism.

As a critique of liberalism, Marxism is trenchant. Its crucial flaw is that it does not criticize, but merely reformulates, the faith that has brought us to our present impasse. It accepts the activist faith of modern man. It purports only to show how the human will can—or in the course of human history will—learn to avoid individual and class fragmentation, thus finally becoming truly effective. The tragedies of history are tacitly reduced to the enmity of man and nature, thus safeguarding the self-confidence already instilled by liberalism. Nature will in time be subdued through intelligent action—first through the technological development brought about by capitalism, then, when the necessary conditions have come into being, through a social and political reformation placing technology at the service of all humankind.

Marxist collectivism is a restatement, not a departure from, the modern faith. There is no doubt much to be said for this collectivism. Businessmen have been spontaneously collectivist in creating the great corporations. For society as a whole to retain its individualism would be to ignore the character of the world—to acquiesce in a contradiction of fact and principle which may serve the immediate interests of businessmen but leaves society as a whole unrepresented and unprotected. Collective will, however, is no less will than is individual will. Collectivism is a doctrine of human mastery. Unguided by a sense of destiny, it must be as fateful as the liberal doctrine of individualistic mastery. It is no less blind to the plenitude of reality or to the limits and imperfections of humanity. Hence it is often ineffective or despotic, and sometimes it is both. The torrent of suffering that has engulfed the Russian people since 1917 has many causes; but that it has all been presided over by a Marxist government is not accidental.

Granting ultimacy to human will, Marxism leads as readily to class conflict as does liberalism. Marxist classes are apt to be thoroughly political: on one side officials, on the other side legally disciplined workers. They are classes, nonetheless, definable in social and economic, as well as political, terms and their existence is owing to the same circumstance that is the basic cause of class divisions in liberal societies: the power and prevalence of will. Will effects subordination, of nature to man and of man to man. A political doctrine that enthrones the will, whether individually or collectively, necessarily gives rise to patterns of domination.

Marxist willfulness reaches its height in the doctrine and practice of revolution. Although Marx was far from an impetuous revolutionary (his entire teaching might be understood as a painstaking definition of the conditions of successful revolution), the animus of his doctrine and life was revolutionary. To change the world, not simply to understand it, was the point. But there is almost nothing in modern experience to substantiate Marx's faith that there are conditions under which human will can be fully effective through revolution. Modern large-scale revolutions have almost invariably become, not merely harsh and murderous, but independent of the will of the original revolutionaries. The pride, not only of Marx but of modern man as well, comes to a climax in the idea that humankind can deliberately and swiftly transform society, and the fate attending revolutionary efforts has been of proportionate scale and severity.

In the philosophies of Marxists and liberals alike the failures of modern man are attributed to temporary weakness. With the progress of technology and social science this weakness will be overcome, whether by society organized collectively or by enterprising individuals. This faith, however, ignores a truth which, once noted, can hardly be denied: that man's weakness is inherent in his finitude. Some kinds of weakness are due to historical circumstances, but some are ontological. The failures of modern man originate in an unwillingness to recognize his ontological weakness. This is to say that our situation is not fundamentally economic or political, but moral. The struggle with nature is but the form in which we witness a struggle taking place within the soul, a struggle in which a disposition to be divine, knowing and commanding all things, is striving to suppress a disposition to be merely human, realizing the paradoxical glory that can be found in freely accepted finitude. The more modest disposition has been little heard from in the age of industrialism and revolution, but it has not died out. It is the call of destiny, and it has a strange—albeit dangerous—ally in fate. If fate does not destroy us it may, by forcing us to pause and reflect, help to awaken us to the nature and requirements of our humanity.

Summarizing, modern man has no answer to the fragmentation of history except the application of will—the individual will of liberals or the collective will of Marxists. Relying on will, however, means ignoring destiny and magnifying fate. Our alienation from the past and future is deepened. This is the impasse in which we stand today. In order better to understand this impasse, let us examine it in terms of the principles by means of which will seeks supremacy.

WILL AND PROPERTY

Will is ordinarily expressed in principles. This is because principles provide assurance of mastery—however illusory the assurance may be. It is true that someone supremely self-confident and ambitious might yearn for mastery of a kind uninhibited even by principles. But most people feel more securely in control of things if they think that valid rules of action are in their possession. Hence the "scholasticism" of revolutionary organizations—the intense involvement in doctrinal development, the respect accorded "theoreticians."

The principles of greatest concern in recent centuries have been those of property, principles regulating ownership. The reason for this is that the will to mastery, where it is assumed that all human beings ought to be free and unmastered, is necessarily concentrated on physical nature. In an era of liberty, equality, and fraternity, will must be applied primarily to the earth. Principles of property determine control of the earth. Of course possession of property entails control of human beings as well as of physical nature. This is true whether property is individual or collective. The power inherent in property is readily ignored, however, as is shown by the air of injured innocence with which both capitalists and communists respond to criticism based on the inhuman consequences of their property systems.

Hence the problem of historical mastery becomes for modern man the problem of the earth and its ownership. The effort to overcome the fragmentation of history embroils us in questions of property and possession. Technology provides only the means for domination. Property systems decide who shall exercise those means. If the physical universe is to be under human control, property must be in the right hands. Whose are the right hands?

The number of possible answers is infinite. All, however, are variations on one or the other, or a combination, of the alternatives embodied in the time-honored issue of private *versus* public ownership. Brief consideration of this issue will bring into view the essential point: just as the human will is weak ontologically, so all principles that would empower the will are essentially inadequate.

The two sides take their stands on common ground— ground that gives an apparent advantage to the defenders of public ownership. It is widely granted that in some primal, perhaps mystical, sense the earth belongs to all of us in common. "The heaven, even the heavens," according to the Bible, "are the Lord's: but the earth hath he given to the children of men."[5] This presumably means, as it was taken even by one of the most influential of all defenders of private property, John Locke, to mean, that the earth belongs to "Mankind in common."[6] As an abstract principle, apart from its practical applications, this is a nearly irresistible moral intuition. It appeals compellingly to our sense that destiny is universally human and that the setting in which destiny is fulfilled, the earth, is the common possession of the human race.

But what does this mean in practice? How can the human race actually take the earth into its possession? According to Locke, only through individual appropriation. The only way in which the earth can be effectively used is for individuals, serving as surrogates for humankind, to take portions of it into their possession: an argument which invites a cynical response but is not insubstantial. As a way of exploiting the natural wealth of the earth, and even of distributing industrial products widely, American capitalism is a striking success.

A more important consideration is moral, that of protecting the individual. Presumably it is a common interest of the human race to use the earth in a way which will safeguard the integrity of persons. This points toward private ownership. Would free personal life be possible without articles of use and places of withdrawal to which individuals can enforce their claims even against majorities and governments? Exponents of public ownership do not ordinarily seek the destruction of small-scale property, but their central argument is likely to obscure its importance. And they do not lay to rest the doubt whether, without private property large enough in scale to be capable of resisting governmental power, small-scale private property could survive.

It has long been apparent, however, that the principle of private ownership is potentially fateful. Professed and applied unreservedly, it is productive of harsh and unjust inequalities, economic instability, and wanton despoliation of nature. And as already pointed out, if economic decisions all are made in numerous independent places, without central planning and control, the result is bound to be a relatively autonomous economic order, insubordinate to human purposes. One of the most fateful events of modern times was the Depression of 1929. This was produced by specifiable human activities, yet these were so spontaneous and scattered that the collapse of industries and banks and the spread of unemployment seemed as independent of human foresight and will as a plague.

Such failures, however, are only practical manifestations of a crucial moral flaw in the principle of private property: it demands nothing from our common humanity. It protects and sanctions a devotion to private values that is destructive of the consciousness of destiny. Even if the argument for laissez-faire, by which uninhibited use of private property is reconciled with the public good, were valid, it still would be unacceptable, for it promises wealth and justice without moral effort. It is fortunate that capitalism does not work as well as it is supposed to. We would be tempted to put ourselves in the hands of a benevolent fate.

It is not surprising that the principle of public ownership has been passionately advanced. It rests on two great pillars: failures that can be traced back to the principle of private ownership, and the immense moral force of the idea that the earth belongs to "the children of men." For Marx, the one key measure for overcoming the alienation present in industrial society is the abolition of private property. This was true even at the time of his early writings, when he seemed more inclined to rely on human spontaneity than on objective principles. And today, after a century of historical experience of a kind that might have been designed to turn us all into cynics, the idea of public ownership tends just by bare enunciation to win support from idealists and to silence doubts.

A simple but serious question, however, faces defenders of public ownership: what does it mean? The truth is that we do not know how the children of men can take possession of the earth—assuming that Locke's answer is unsatisfactory. There have been countless schemes but none have been proven in practice and none come near to being intellectually irresistible. So far as we know, the only effective alternative to individual appropriation is governmental appropriation, and governments are not better surrogates for humankind than are owners of private property. This leaves us arguing the relative advantages of private and governmental ownership, and in this argument the former side is, as we have seen, far from defenseless.

Equated with *governmental* ownership, the principle of public ownership promotes extreme concentration of power; economic and political power are in the same hands. This in turn encourages massive and unchecked assertions of will. The results are apt to be as fateful as those following from assertions of will on the part of multitudes of unchecked and self-seeking private individuals—particularly when governments controlling economic resources are in the hands of individuals who are heedless of the disadvantages of public ownership. This, of course, will normally be the case. This is at least one of the hidden links in the ironic fate that Soviet despotism, as morally monstrous as any government in history, is based on a principle of property that is morally superior to that ordinarily recognized by the more humane governments of the West.

Practical people have long rejected the extremes of public and private ownership, but they seem usually to believe that there is some correct position between the extremes. Pragmatic liberals look for the "right balance" between the polar principles, and experimental radicals investigate devices, such as participation of workers in management, that will enable humankind to repossess the earth.

No true principle of property exists, however. Every system for apportioning the earth, whether representing one of the polar principles or some combination of them, is bound to be attended by undesirable consequences. We have no way of establishing dominion over the physical universe and every property system will reveal our weakness. Possession of the earth is a possibility hidden in human destiny but not contained in any principles of property. The question is whether we are willing, as Job counselled, to "speak to the earth" and to listen for its teaching—to attend to the concord of man and being that artistic, philosophical, and religious insight has repeatedly disclosed at the roots of physical reality.

Maintaining some particular dogma of property is one of the hallmarks of ideology. It is in the nature of an ideology that it prescribes ultimate and infallible rules of action, thus assuring mastery. Among the prescribed rules of action, those pertaining to the control of physical reality must be preeminent, since human beings are supposed to be free. Hence every ideology provides a program for fashioning the earth in accordance with human goals. This program must assume the form of an ideal property system. If there were no ideal system, people would be forced away from ideology and back into a posture of receptivity.

Property is power and an incitement therefore to willfulness. This is one reason why every property system is inadequate. Private and public ownership, and all combinations of these, inspire the will to command and thus, in various ways, call forth fate. In distributing property, the will to possess the earth—that is, a more or less disguised form of the will to power—merely arranges for its own satisfaction. Today all of this is becoming apparent. The argument between proponents of private and public property, carried on for so long and still unresolved, is being brought to an obvious impasse.

This impasse shapes our present historical situation. Disillusioned with communism, socialism, and the welfare state, unwilling to return to unrestrained capitalism, we see no way of moving ahead. The physical universe, although transformed by human action, stands before us like a set of towering cliffs: a defiled earth, a dehumanizing work system, stultifying wealth. As for the human universe, liberty, equality, and fraternity remain, as Marxists charge, mere ideals, condemning but not determining social and political reality. We sense the vanity of trying to move forward by means of any of the principles of property in which we formerly placed such excessive hope. On the other hand, we do not feel called to any enterprise of self-examination, for we predicated our efforts to attain mastery on our own essential innocence.

We have entered in this way into a crisis of the will. Facing a recalcitrant earth and finding ourselves in opposition to our own ideals, we experience deep frustration. It is commonplace that man is inhuman to man. Modern experience discloses a more complicated and trying truth: that the inhumanity of man comes from a sincere, if proud, effort to be human. It comes from an effort to humanize the earth and to liberate humanity. The crisis toward which yearning for sovereignty over the earth and history has led is reached when it becomes apparent that we must either give up the ideal of sovereignty or else, in one final surge toward dominion, set aside every limitation upon the will. This crisis can be described in terms of a simple alternative—receptivity or nihilism.

THE WILL TO ANNIHILATION

Nihilism is a commitment to destruction. In its extreme manifestations, it is a love of destruction for its own sake. In its relatively moderate forms, it envisions destruction as clearing the ground for the realization of ideals. A constructive purpose, however, is either lacking altogether or is provisionally set aside. Will is freed even of the limits implied by plans and purposes.

To those not profoundly dissatisfied with the whole world around them, nihilism looks like insanity. To the desperate, however, it has a powerful and comprehensible appeal. Inner conflict is ended, for the ideals that condemned and inhibited action are thrown off. The consciousness of guilt, inseparable from allegiance to these ideals, is thrown off at the same time; a nihilist may commit atrocities buoyed by an exhilarating sense of innocence. Pride reaches its greatest heights. One is now superior even to the moral law.

Nihilism does not arise because people are rationally convinced by nihilistic arguments. Indeed, there is a certain incompatibility between the nihilistic and the philosophical temper, although one great philosopher, Friedrich Nietzsche, may be classified as a nihilist. The appeal of nihilism is to passions that grow under the stresses of fate. The crisis of will brought on by these stresses forces a person either to sacrifice or vindicate his pride.

Not everything can be destroyed, so the nihilist vindicates his pride by destroying the supposed sources of all evil. In identifying such sources, in choosing objects for destruction, the irrationality of nihilism is apt to become apparent. It is difficult reasonably to single out any reality or set of realities as the one source of evil. Hence any source that is specified, such as the Jews, is apt to appear fantastic except to those already convinced by hatred. But for people balanced precariously on the edge of violence, a fantasy that offers a release of destructive passions, along with a clear conscience, may be irresistible. Nihilism appeals to those who are desperate to clear themselves of all blame and to aim a devastating blow at everything that frustrates and torments them.

In its extreme forms, nihilism is demonic. The term "demonic" does not mean merely that something is evil. A demonic movement or person is *possessed* by evil. Men like Hitler and Stalin seem to be more (or less) than malicious and powerful individuals. They seem to be embodiments of evil forces, instruments controlled and used by those forces. This is a way of saying that anything demonic is fateful. The irrational fury expressed in nihilism is a manifestation of fate. One senses the presence of fate both in Hitler's melodramatic end, in the flames of Berlin, and in Stalin's death, suffered as he prepared the bloody repression of yet another plot conjured from out of the abyss of his fears.

Although a nihilistic leader may seem possessed by impersonal evil forces, the individual human being is not effaced. Pride remains at the source of fate even when it moves people helplessly to acts of destruction, and pride is always liable to pit self against others. Nihilism may take the form of limitless self-assertion. Dostoevsky describes the terrible conceptual transformation which in the Christian era often underlies demonic pride. The idea of the God-man is changed into that of the man-god. The term is apt in our times. To give Hitler or Stalin the age-old designation of tyrant is accurate but inadequate. The scale of the pretensions of a single human being are better indicated by speaking of human self-deification.

The substitution of the man-god for the God-man explains the objects of nihilistic fury. The penultimate object is the individual so far as the individual is regarded as a possessor of ineluctable dignity. The concept of the God-man was construed in a way that exalted every individual; the concept of the man-god exalts one or a few. The idea of the dignity of every individual places severe limits on will, even to the extent that all political action would be barred if it were interpreted literally and followed exactly. Hence the utmost liberation of will, that most befitting a man-god, is to humiliate and destroy individuals. (In Dostoevsky's terms: if the God-man is an illusion and only the man-god is real, then "all is permitted.") Under nihilistic political regimes people are mistreated not only for utilitarian reasons (such as using them as slave labor), and not only for the satisfaction of the malicious impulses found in every age and society, but simply in order to violate their dignity. The commanders and guards in Hitler's concentration camps did not merely ignore the worth of individuals, but they tried to destroy that worth, to disprove the very idea of it. They systematically humiliated the human person. Perhaps nothing of this sort could have happened except in a civilization that had developed a deep, but also troubled and unstable, respect for the individual.

The ultimate object of nihilistic hatred is transcendence, or God. The man-god cannot exist, as Nietzsche showed with incomparable dramatic force, as long as God exists, or indeed as long as any realm of being surpassing human comprehension and power exists. The nihilistic effort to lay waste the dignity of individuals is in part an assault on God, for the dignity of individuals has been traditionally understood as originating in God.

Nihilism is will at its last extremity. We have seen that the attempted conquest of nature comes to a climax, and fails, in the encounter with death. Man is defeated by nature in dying. Correspondingly, the effort at historical mastery culminates and fails when man becomes not just the victim but the agent of death. Here too man is defeated—but by his own will rather than nature, and not in dying but in killing.

A vision of fate flowing from the fury of the man-god, a fury at once demonic and proud, is cast in allegorical form in a great work of world literature, Herman Melville's *Moby Dick*. In his demonic hunt for the white whale, Ahab is trying to discover and destroy the ultimate mystery of all things. The dignity and lives of individuals, while not the peculiar objects of his hatred, mean nothing to him. The members of his crew are fused into an instrument of his will and are, with a single exception, destroyed. The motive is pride. Ahab is a mountain-peak of self-assertion, living in awful and unapproachable solitude. "In his fiery eyes of scorn and triumph, you . . . saw Ahab in all his fatal pride." To affirm his own separate, integral being Ahab denied all mystery and all that resisted the dominion of his will. "I'd strike the sun," he declared, "if it insulted me."[7]

Ahab was all intrasigence and defiance. Yet he was completely in the thrall of fate and he himself recognized won-deringly that this was so. "What is it," he demanded, "what nameless, inscrutable, unearthly thing is it; what cozzening, hidden lord and master, and cruel, remorseless emperor com-mands me; that against all natural lovings and longings, I so keep pushing, and crowding, and jamming myself on all the time; recklessly making me ready to do what in my own proper, natural heart, I durst not so much as dare?"[8] In this coincidence of furious will and fateful helplessness we can see the essence of the demonic. And we can see modern man on the outermost boundaries of his world, maddened by his consciousness that the will to mastery has reached its limits and that he is in a position not of sovereignty but of bondage. "We are turned round and round in this world, like yonder windlass," Ahab laments, "and Fate is the handspike."[9]

6

THE TRUE POLITICAL ART

DESTINY AND POLITICS

WHEN FATE IS ASCENDANT, politics is bound to be unattractive. It will appear futile. If events are hopelessly out of control, governing is necessarily a useless activity. It is likely also to be corrupt. Appearing futile, it is bound to be dispiriting, and those involved in it may be more than ordinarily inclined to counterbalance the dissatisfactions inherent in their tasks with the satisfactions of wealth and privilege.

Our situation and our state of mind today are not unlike those of the Greeks after the downfall of the city-state. Now as then history seems deadly and incomprehensible. In Greece certain philosophers condemned political life because of the useless cares it entailed and urged people to "live unknown." One powerful school, the Epicurean, advised people to devote their lives to pleasure, or at least to the minimization of pain. It could be said that present-day industrial societies are inhabited mainly by practicing Epicureans. Almost everyone is preoccupied with the satisfactions thought to be found in industrial abundance. The major public institutions scarcely pretend to fulfill any function except that of ministering to this purpose. Life is essentially private, as Epicurus asserted that it should be. Correspondingly, many look on politics, with Epicurus' skepticism, as unrelated to any serious human interests.

It would be a mistake to dismiss such attitudes as merely cynical or selfish, either among the avowed Epicureans of ancient times or among the tacit Epicureans of the present day. Epicurus was morally serious and highly civilized, and for many people of antiquity his doctrine was a sober and seemingly saving way of life. And anyone who considers even for a moment all of the ways modern governments have failed—through miscalculation, timidity, corruption, and cruelty—will have to admit that contemporary Epicureans are not unreasonable. The fated governments of our time, large, action-oriented, and ineffective, invite a repudiation of politics.

Nevertheless, a position already reached in the course of these reflections rules out the idea that living well requires or even allows withdrawal from politics. It is ruled out by what has been said about the relationship of destinies. I cannot regard my own destiny as an altogether exceptional gift. I am bound to think that others, perhaps all others, are given destinies, and I am compelled by respect for my own destiny to respect these other possible destinies. This is a matter not only of logic but of experience. Just as my own personal life at its most creative is a venture in communication, so I experience my destiny as lived with others and even, in some sense, as the same destiny that others live. If I am imaginative, I may feel at moments that I am living the destiny of all humankind. Correspondingly, in entering into relations with others, not only do I see traces of destiny in their lives (especially in the lives of those I love or of great historical figures), but I sometimes see that destiny as my own.

This is to speak of the universality of destiny, of the idea that destiny is at once intimately personal and universally human. If love is a recognition of destiny, then the scriptural command to love one's neighbor as oneself implies the universality of destiny, for one's neighbor can be anyone. The Epicurean ideal of withdrawal is a denial of this universality. If destiny is universally human, then turning away from the affairs of the human race and concentrating on one's own private concerns is a rejection of destiny. There was a fatal incongruity in Epicurus' effort to give weight and significance to private life by ignoring the life of the world around.

It is true that Epicurus praised personal friendship. Private life was not the same as solitude. But if friendship depends on a recognition of destiny in one's friends, and if destiny is universal, then friendship abstracted from all responsibility in relation to the whole human race is impossible.

This argument can be cast in terms of history. To be available for one's destiny it is necessary consciously to live in time. Destiny is temporal and requires one to accept the temporality of existence. Only by inhabiting time lucidly and unreservedly is one present, so to speak, in the sphere of destiny. Although destiny is given by transcendence, it is not given to those who try deliberately to exalt themselves above time. It is not merely personal time that must be accepted, however, but historical time. Time must be understood in accordance with the universality of destiny— as history. Only by living consciously and responsibly in history can one be fully receptive to human destiny and hence to his own destiny in particular.

The history of all people and all ages is a concept disquieting in its vastness and apparent impersonality. The notion that it concerns in any way the single individual was derided by Kierkegaard. But the idea of history as universal and meaningful did not arise in minds indifferent to "the existing individual" whom Kierkegaard so tenaciously and brilliantly championed. It was formulated, originally with Augustine, as an expression of the faith that even the most insignificant of individuals had a destiny determined by eternity and invulnerable to temporal accidents. The secret of universal history, it followed, must lie in personal destinies. Just as Plato saw the structure of the individual soul written in large letters in the state, Augustine saw the destiny of the individual outlined in the drama of world events from the earliest to the final ages. Thus to say that receptivity to a destiny requires one to be situated consciously and responsibly within historical time does not call on us to be occupied with something alien and distant but only to recognize the true nature and range of the life each person tries to live.

As appropriate as it may be, however, for the conformations of individual consciousness and responsibility to be historical, it is not easy. This is not so much because of the scale of world history; human imagination is able to envision the unity of all times and places if there is a real desire to do so. The difficulty of inhabiting history is owing more to the anxiety of living in time. As destined beings we are wanderers, or pilgrims, unable to live in permanent settlements. Inhabiting history, we realize that every lasting order, from the order of the home to that of the state, is continually being changed and is inevitably moving toward dissolution. The wandering of the ancient Jewish tribes, free of the enslaving security of Egypt, but spending decades in the wilderness on the way to the destination promised them by God, is a myth that illuminates our obligations. The powers of the world conspire unremittingly to stifle historical consciousness. They do this for the sake of the power and wealth they can gain by inducing us to settle down and enjoy ourselves. Not only capitalists but socialists as well urge us toward conditions of economic comfort and security that would militate against the receptivity and movement without which no destiny can be realized. All ideologies claim to show how historical time can be mastered or in some way transcended. A concern for destiny demands that all visions of world-fixity (whether the world be a private home or a nation) be resisted.

In summary, to be prepared to live a destiny one must be related consciously and responsibly to all destinies and hence to history. This is a way of restating the old theme that to a human being no other human beings, of any place or time, are insignificant. Does this principle, however, fully counter Epicurus? Does it mandate a political relationship with others?

I understand politics to be the conduct of our lives in common. If this is so, a relationship with others that is comprehensive (with all human beings, on the basis of all major components of a good life) and responsible (prepared for choice and action wherever these are appropriate) is political. To cultivate a consciousness of global problems and of their historical dimensions, and deliberately to assume and defend a position in relation to these problems, is to adopt a political stance. And to inquire into our common problems and to act upon or endure them, according to circumstances, and so far as possible in company with others, is to take part in politics. This does not necessarily mean holding office or working with organizations; here everything depends on personality and situation. A governmental official whose thoughts were only of carrying out established routines or of garnering personal honor would be non-political; a janitor or schoolteacher whose tasks were fulfilled as acts of conscious participation in the affairs of common life would be political. What is crucial is inhabiting as articulately and deliberately as possible the entire human situation—being positioned, inquiringly and communally, in relation to the great problems of one's own historical era.

It must be granted that the most unsparing battles against fate often go on in solitude and not in political gatherings. But the only victory in these battles is in discovering and living a destiny that is human, that is ours as well as mine, and the only hopeful struggle against fate is carried on—perhaps in the utmost solitude—in behalf of all. Our loss of political bearings and habits is a sign of our having been overwhelmed by fate. If we are to keep our footing, our accessibility to destiny, we must gain a political consciousness that is without fanaticism but is also, as a consciousness of common and responsible humanity, unyielding. The art of doing this is "the true political art."

This is not, however, what most people today think of as the political art. To understand it we must think further about the nature of politics. We may do this advantageously by examining the concept of order. From the time of Plato to the present it has been widely assumed that the purpose of political action and the object of political thought is just and propitious order. This assumption is neither so inevitable nor so innocuous as it seems.

POLITICS AND ORDER

Were we to carry forward these reflections in terms of order, the ideal would be that of a receptive society, of a political and social order open to the discernment and living of destinies. This would be an order open toward transcendence and favoring, therefore, the serious dialogical relationships through which human beings orient themselves toward transcendence. As for the kind of order that would be, much would depend on circumstances. But the general conditions that encourage transcendental and communal openness are so apparent that they hardly need to be mentioned. People ought to be protected from poverty of a severity that reduces life to the level of physical necessity; they ought to be educated in a way calculated to enhance both their capacity and their respect for thought and discourse; they ought to enjoy legally protected freedom of communication such as that secured in the United States through the First Amendment. These might be considered the axioms of political receptivity.

To attach very much significance to such prescriptions, however, would be to think in terms that must be questioned. The notion that all political activity and thought should center on order is based on assumptions that are widespread and enduring but deserve, nevertheless, to be examined. These assumptions might be summarized as follows.

(1) The ideal order can be known and described, perhaps in the form of a utopia, or else as a systematic set of clear and unconditional rules of justice and statecraft.

(2) A person achieves full humanity through inhabiting an ideal order. Harmony of the soul, and in consequence happiness, is derived from the harmony of the surrounding order.

(3) An ideal order can be established. Human beings are wise and good enough for that task, and often a specific historical entity (a party, class, or nation) can be counted on to further the realization of the ideal order.

(4) Anyone willing to give time and effort can probably make a significant contribution to the establishment of the ideal. The average person can be an appreciable force in political affairs.

These assumptions, in various forms and degrees, are shared by all political creeds. Liberals, radicals, and conservatives differ in their definitions of ideal order and in the identification of favoring institutions and historical forces; they differ in their views of the source and character of our knowledge of order and its requirements. But the notion that ideal order is humanly conceivable and attainable, and constitutes the central issue of political thought and life, marks out not a particular political persuasion, but rather the overall area within which all major political persuasions are situated.

All four assumptions, nonetheless, are almost certainly false. They are so prevalent and durable, and appear so indubitable, because they are rarely questioned and not because they are particularly strong or even, from every point of view, very plausible.

(1) The requirements of ideal order in any given situation are usually in conflict. For example, justice presumably requires that values be distributed in accordance both with need and with contribution to the common good. But these do not necessarily coincide; the needs of someone who is seriously ill may be great and the capacity for contributing to the common good nil. Which standard, then, is prior? The impulses of idealism suggest that need is prior to desert. But socialist and other reformist efforts in recent decades, and mere common sense as well, make it clear that an economy which considers only need, and neglects the rewards expected and in some sense deserved by those who work, manage, and invest, probably will not produce enough to satisfy even the needy, much less the deserving. Another example is provided by the conflict of equality and command. The ideal of community requires that people meet in unreserved openness, free of pre-established hierarchies and ulterior designs. Social necessities, however, dictate that some assume posi-

tions of power over others, sometimes deceiving and coercing them to attain the ends of the group. Here again principle clashes with principle. How can such conflicts be decided? Not by any superordinate principle. Not only are the ideal and the practical often dissonant, but ideals may be dissonant with one another and practical counsels clash. Such dissonance nullifies every claim to even general certainty, based on principle, as to what ought to be done in any concrete situation. Every comprehensive social ideal, every systematic set of social norms, is a ship that is sure to founder sometime before the historical journey on which it carries us is ended.

Every actual order, then, is imperfect. The imperfections of order are infinite in detail but definable in their general form. Limits are necessarily placed on personal behavior; those limits must be defined and enforced by some in relation to others; and such arrangements entail alienation, not only between the powerful and the powerless but among the powerful and among the powerless as well. In short, every order is constraining, inegalitarian, and estranging—in conflict with liberty, equality, and fraternity (or community). The constraints, inequalities, and distances do not result merely from the errors of framers of constitutions and leaders of governments—although such failures occur again and again in the history of every polity and greatly exacerbate the imperfections of every established order. The best possible order would be seriously defective and hence would in some way violate our highest ideals. Accordingly, it must be said that man and order are incongruous.

(2) This being so, humanity is not achieved by inhabiting an ideal order, for there is no such order. What if there were? Even so, I suggest, there would be a moral disparity between order and the individual human being. It is difficult to speak on this matter with complete assurance because we cannot be confident that we grasp all the implications of the concept of ideal order; perhaps its realization presupposes ontological changes, such as the alteration or abolition of space and time, that would render our usual concepts and methods

of reflection inapplicable. Assuming, however, that our present ontological situation does not incapacitate us for reflecting on this subject, it may be said that order and personality apparently belong to different levels of being. Order belongs on the level of objectivity and rationality; in Kantian terms, it is phenomenal. Personality is noumenal. Order entails regularity (this is true both of physical and moral order), personality, freedom. The desire to enter into realities larger than the self reflects a nisus toward community, not toward order. This is to take issue with Plato and with attitudes represented in practically all ancient Hellenic thought. It is to invoke the sense of personality implanted in the Western mind mainly by Christianity and expressed dramatically in Augustine, the sense that a human being contains rationally incomprehensible depths. If that intuition is accurate, even a perfect order cannot, as Plato suggests it might, be a human being "writ large."

(3) As for the claim that human beings have the capacity at last and in spite of all obstacles to establish an ideal order, no one can prove the contrary. The issue is the persistence and power of pride and despair—of "sin." Those who envision man as a potential creator of ideal order necessarily construe human perversities as temporary and relative. In view of the millenia of disorder behind us and of the human traits most conspicuous in our own age of disorder, however, that interpretation must be regarded as a daring act of faith rather than a reasonable calculation. Granted, faith of some kind is necessary if life is to have glory or even serenity. But faith in what? Mistaken faith is absolute reliance on something that is sure to fail. Hence acts of faith demand, paradoxically, a critical and cautious mind. Exalting man is exhilarating but belongs, all evidence suggests, among our more uncritical and dangerous acts of faith.

All of this has implications bearing on the trust we put in institutions and historical forces. Absolute reliance on an institution fits exactly the archetype of misplaced faith, that is, idolatry, for it is faith in something man-made. Reliance on some historical force usually means trusting in a mental faculty (faith in progress, for example, is basically faith in reason) or in a group (perhaps the working class) which has not congealed institutionally but comes no nearer to absolute reliability than any institution. Everyone recalls the title of a book published a generation ago by several former Communists: *The God That Failed*. The Communist party is not the only god that has failed in recent times. The disappointments, terrors, and tragedies of our century indicate that the best human institutions, the most constructive mental faculties, and the most beneficent historical forces, all are morally ambiguous, containing possibilities of evil as well as of good.

(4) Although certain particular individuals in every historical era have a significant effect on the course of events, these are necessarily exceptions. It must be remembered that we are speaking of the movement of history. In the nature of things the contribution that the average individual singly can make to ideal order, or to any other historical goal, is infinitesimal. Collectively, it is true, individuals determine events; this does not affect the fact that I, personally, have no perceptible influence. With respect to historical results, my decisions and actions are irrelevant. In the democracies, where supposedly every vote counts, we are reluctant to acknowledge the historical insignificance of the average individual. But once noted, that insignificance is too plain to be disputed.

Summarizing, it might be said that we are in the habit of looking on order as a collective artifact. As such, it can be perfectly constructed and we must all join in the task of seeing that it is. The analogy is more fitting still if we see such an artifact as architectural, an ideal habitation for humanity. Such a conception perhaps is natural to a civilization preoccupied for some generations now with technological fabrication. What happens if this habit is cast aside?

The question before us changes. No longer do we ask above all else, How should things be arranged? With greater urgency we ask, What should I do? In a world in which ideal order is inconceivable, and, even if conceivable, not a fitting home for humanity nor susceptible of realization, a world moreover in which my personal influence is negligible, how should I conduct myself? I may think about and work for the best practicable order, but that cannot encompass my political responsibilities. I must take into account my situation, denied any actual or ideal home in history, without any absolutely reliable historical allies, and without significant power. I must face problems such as maintaining a critical detachment in relation to all ideals, institutions, and historical forces, entering into relations with others that are not defined in terms of an ideal order, and acting responsibly in view of the fact that my acts are historically inconsequential. A critique of order forces us to recast our definitions of political responsibility. Even if the concept of order retains an important place in those definitions, it is necessarily dethroned. It is subordinated to the question of how I, alone in history and weak, should conduct my life.

A broad answer emerges clearly from this essay: I should live my destiny. The primary task of a human being is not to devise plans for saving the human race. It is to care for the soul. Individual responsibility must be conceived on a scale commensurate with the limitations of individual power. This, however, is not to repudiate political responsibility. As shown in the preceding section, availability for a destiny requires the whole range of relationships that is implicit in adopting a genuine political stance. Care of the soul is at once deeply personal and thoroughly political. Combining these two attitudes is not easy but it is possible. It is a matter of practicing "the true political art."

This phrase originated with Socrates, who said that he himself was the only Athenian who practiced the true political art. Socrates lived amid a people absorbed as few peoples have been in political rivalries and plans. Socrates himself was hardly involved in politics of this sort at all. He cared nothing for official status and showed little interest in day-to-day political issues. Not only did he remain aloof from political struggles, he was viewed with mistrust by his fellow citizens. In what sense, then, can the conduct of his life be called a political art?

In Socrates' stance two characteristics, apparently logical opposites, yet in truth interdependent, are dramatically evident. (It may help one to see these characteristics as political to note that they pertain also to a familiar American political figure, Abraham Lincoln.) First, Socrates was a solitary figure. We can only think of him as living through the climax of his destiny alone, spending his last hours with friends, yet marked off from them not just by the proximity of his death but by his incomprehensible cheerfulness. (Lincoln was ridiculed from every side, even by members of his cabinet, and was highly esteemed by scarcely anyone except the ordinary men and women of the country.) At the same time, Socrates was an eminently communicative man. His readiness to listen and speak was not merely an inclination or habit but entered into the essence of his personality. His very destiny lay in dialogue. (Lincoln, although a war leader, presiding over a conflict rare in scale and ferocity, found himself thus in circumstances tragically antithetical to his sociable and compassionate temper.) To understand the true political art, the political responsibilities required by destiny, we must envision these two characteristics combined.

SOLITARY COMMUNALITY, OR CIVILITY

The phrase "solitary communality" indicates succinctly the posture of a person awaiting his destiny in the presence of fate. The phrase is paradoxical and it suggests a difficult personal balance. In a civilization aggressively social and organizational but inwardly desolate, however, solitude and communality both are imperative and belong together. This will become apparent as we examine each attitude separately.

The individual before fate is solitary. Fate sets people apart from one another. It may bind them together in giant organizations but in doing this it equates them with what is calculable and manageable in their personalities and thus falsi- fies them and precludes communal relationships. It renders them, even if organizationally fused, fundamentally alone. This is an aspect of the irony of fate. Bureaucrats, business executives, party leaders, and other agents of fate aspire to unite people totally; in fact they divide them through the processes of objectification to which their aims commit them.

Nothing is worse in this situation than for individuals to convince themselves that some particular historical entity, such as a state or a party, provides a way of evading or conquering fate. It is tempting to do this. The ancient Greeks saw the city-state as a tiny realm of freedom which, as seemed to be triumphantly proven at Marathon, could provide a haven for humanity in a world dominated by vast and fateful empires. And Christians have often recoiled from a fallen world, seeking refuge in a church providentially purified and set apart from the world; Augustine responded to one of the most fateful of historical events, the fall of the Roman Empire, by affirming the destiny of the Catholic Church. In our own time many have sought solid ground, firm amidst confused spiritual tides, in totalitarian states and parties. Not that every refuge must be wholly spurned; to have been a citizen of early fifth-century Athens must have been a rare blessing of fortune. But people show a persistent inclination to sanctify their places of refuge, thus treating a mere historical entity as perfect and holy.

To be available for destiny, each one must accept and live through a solitary confrontation with fate. This means keep- ing all historical idols at a distance, entering into only the most guarded relationships with ideologies, leaders, and parties. It means asserting tenaciously one's moral autonomy, refusing to allow any authority to preempt the continuing task—the Socratic task!—of moral reflection and decision. Some of the most moving examples of this resolute disen- gagement are seen among exiles and political prisoners. But such conduct is not for exiles alone. No one can be faithful to his own being in times when fate is ascendant without living as an inward exile, disengaged in his own country, even if this is done in ways so inconspicuous as to be hardly discernible to an observer.

One of the hardest demands of solitude is doing without honor—without recognition and praise from others. Supposedly a person needs to be recognized as the one he really is. Perhaps so, if "need" be understood as something very much wanted but not indispensable. However, society is almost always too blind and impersonal to meet the need for recognition, and to affirm that need as absolute is to prepare the way for social idolatry. One must live the life that is given to one to live and must do this without depending on the sanction of any other person or any group. One must do this, moreover, without assurance that sanction, or recognition, will come in time. To live lucidly without honor is to accept not only the state of being ignored but the prospect of being everlastingly forgotten. It is to enter willingly into a state of social oblivion and not to mistake this for ontological destruction. Destiny imposes this test repeatedly, demanding in the most varied and unexpected ways that one make and adhere to the distinction between honor and life.

If Socrates is a historical example of the solitude that a recognition of our historical condition requires, Joseph K., from Kafka's novel *The Trial*, might be seen as a fictional example. Joseph K. is subjected to accusations which he is unable to clarify, rebut, or trace to their source. The situation in which this places him may be interpreted as social, juridical, or religious. What particularly concerns us here is his response to that situation. He does not assume that a society in which he will feel perfectly at home can be created, and he does not join with like-minded comrades to create such a society. Rather, he accepts the fact that he has been set apart, justly or not, by the accusations against him. He seeks help from various others but does not delude himself with thoughts of a sacred refuge. Confused and unsure as he is, he is stubbornly independent.

Also, he is stubbornly rational; that is the source of his independence. Until his death, he inquires unceasingly into the charges against him. "The only thing for me to go on doing," he says, "is to keep my intelligence calm and analytical to the end."[1] Such rationality is closely allied with the second quality exemplified in Socrates, communality.

Although Socrates was so defiant of reigning opinion that he finally provoked Athens to kill him, he was in his defiance invincibly communal. He manifested his independence in speech. And he was not disputatious, establishing his selfhood by arousing antagonism in others. He was dialogical and seemed to live only in conversation. To think of Socrates is to think of a man engaged in common inquiry.

In connection with his communality, the political character of Socrates' life can be seen. The subjects that interested Socrates were not, as I have said, issues of public policy. Rather they were issues of moral character—the nature of virtues such as courage and friendship. The unstated aim of his conversations was to show that his interlocutors, and all who governed and guided Athens, were morally ignorant—unacquainted with the good in its various forms—and in this way to induce them to discard their false opinions and enter into dialogue, the one path to truth. This was political activity in that an understanding of the good is the only basis for public policy and can be gained only by those who have been humbled by being deprived of their illusions. Socrates' political art consisted in educating people for communicative inquiry into common, or political, ends.

In his communality, as in his independence, Socrates can help us envision the stance necessary for facing fate. Communication is a requirement of love, the power by which, in imagination and hope, one liberates the world from fate. Love requires communication above all else. Love that is expressed in physical help alone is demeaning, for such love as that is bestowed even on animals. On the other hand, communication without love—communication confined, for example, to an elite—is arrogant and apt to be fateful in its consequences. Only through love that listens and speaks, through communication that cherishes those heard and addressed, can one be fully accessible to a destiny.

To listen and speak in a way that is morally significant, however, is to listen for the truth and to try to speak the truth. Serious communication is inquiry, and the supreme expression of love is sharing as fully as possible in the search for truth. This is a highly personal enterprise even though truth belongs to all of us and must be sought in common. Truth is personal but not private. In seeking the truth one tries to clarify the configurations of one's life, of destiny. Truth that does not do this, an isolated bit of knowledge concerning chemistry, for example, is insignificant. Our ultimate aim in all serious inquiry is to glimpse the Logos, the destiny that we all share but that each one must enact in a singular life.

We would not realize the severity of destiny, however, if we failed to note that truth is elusive and that few are perseveringly interested in it. Communality is often waiting— rather than listening *to* others, listening *for* them; rather than actually speaking, cultivating in solitude the veracity and sense of responsibility that spells a readiness to speak should a listener be encountered. Love assumes the form of attentiveness and availability.

It can now be seen that solitude and communality constitute a single stance—a communal readiness, in opposition to fate. Solitude is a dedication to possibilities of community that are threatened by established forms of social interaction. Strangely, then, solitude and communality are linked. Through the absolute commitments often made and glorified in our time, a social or political entity is treated as though it were a perfect community. Solitude is thus done away with; but communality also is destroyed, for idolatry replaces attentiveness and availability. Solitude signifies a refusal to enter into fraudulent communities and is consequently a communal state. It is not an end in itself, however, but is intended to create and guard a space for community.

The stance of solitary communality is essential to community, to an inquiring or dialogical life in common. How essential it is is apparent in a fateful era such as ours. It is needed in times of any kind, however, and would be needed even in a dialogical paradise, as a power inherent in a communal being. Community can come into existence only in proportion to the capacity of participants for independent attentiveness and availability. Hence this virtue, which I have already referred to as "the true political art," may for the sake of convenience be called "civility."

But do not these terms—"political art," "civility"—suggest something more than solitude and communality?

CIVILITY AND ACTION

Civility involves a humility and weakness that has little appeal for modern man and is incongruous in the modern world. Surrounded by monuments to human technological genius, it is difficult to bear in mind the unreliability of every human power and institution. It is difficult to remember that our supreme task is not to change the world but to avoid the stultification of absolute commitments and to hold ourselves available for those inquiring relationships in which we may discover purposes that would justify our technological powers.

Such humility and weakness, however, do not entail withdrawal and hopelessness. They constitute the bearing of one who inquires persistently into fate in its full historical massiveness and who hopes for a transfigured society. They underlie the effort to discover what our humanity requires of us. In this way they lay the only possible foundation for humane and fruitful action.

Action is an obligation for anyone attempting to live a destiny. As was seen in chapter 2, action enters indispensably into the definition of a self. Only someone who deliberately and lucidly acts becomes, not merely a representative of the human race in general, but a particular human being, finite and fallible. Only where possible action is at stake can communication be fully serious, that is, common inquiry into human destiny.

It must be granted, therefore, that civility is not solitude and communality alone. These define a state in which one is open not only to the truth but also to actions that truth may require. As already noted, the question which calls forth and shapes the civil stance is, What must I do? Or, to put this in terms of an earlier formulation, one asks, For what was I born? One searches for the necessity that guides legitimate action.

When conceived of and entered into from a stance of solitary communality, action tends to be freed from the moral distortions which affect it in most circumstances. People engaged in action readily exaggerate their own power and virtue while neglecting the full being and value of the realities they are trying to control. Nothing could wholly eradicate the disposition to do this, but solitary communality tends to moderate it.

First, as action in which an individual engages because it presents itself as morally necessary, even if not practically promising, it removes the incubus of historical insignificance which must weigh on an individual placing himself in the stream of historical affairs. As a consequence, the temptations to entertain illusions of human power, whether collective or individual, are greatly lessened. One is not trying to redeem the human race or even necessarily to affect the course of history but only to live a destiny. Outstanding examples of civil action purged of pride are provided by young Germans who resisted Hitler and died without accomplishing anything of historical significance or even being recognized for their courage.

Further, solitary communality instills in action an unwillingness to resolve political responsibility into some simple and unconditional commitment. That kind of commitment is appealing in the twentieth century because it puts solitude and uncertainty behind us. Civility, however, means resisting evil in the form not only of old, neglected problems but also in the form of the monstrous ideological and institutional simplifications that falsely promise to liquidate those problems. Civility is a persistent refusal of idolatry. The world of politics contains some of the most alluring of false gods. If civility consists partly in a commitment to communal inquiry, it consists correspondingly in an insistence that all political gods be exposed to such inquiry. Thus communality toward human beings combines with skepticism toward human works. Resolved on the most searching kind of communication, it permits nothing to stand in the way of transcendence.

The objection might be made that action so rooted in an individual's sense of the requirements of his own life is almost doomed to be historically ineffective. For the course of events to respond to human impulse, individuals must either acquiesce in the acts of leaders or merge their feelings of individual life in a passion of collective life, such as nationalism.

There is perhaps some truth in this objection. We should remember, however, that history cannot be steadily subordinated to any human impulse. The notion that it can is at the origins of fate. Action energized by exaggerated impressions of human power or by idolatry has brought many of our troubles. It is not clear that history would take a turn for the worse were the fervor and drama of collective action to disappear. But the case for civil action may be put more positively.

To be civil is to be alert to the promptings of destiny. If civility suddenly spread throughout a society, the result might be an enhanced capacity for action. Leaders and people might become more clearly aware of the needs of the moment. And ideals—the needs of eternity, so to speak—might recover their vitality. Liberty, equality, and community do not produce results automatically, like chemicals in a human body. They are effective only if they are apprehended by human minds, and they are beneficent only if they are apprehended as symbols of destiny. The latter cannot happen except among human beings capable of solitude and communication. The idea of civility does not postulate political failure. It implies only that we should refrain from counting on political success and should realize that destiny may unfold and history have meaning even when political intentions are frustrated. At its best, civility is a readiness for results which are not historically visible—results occurring in the realm of spirit, not of Caesar. But it does not preclude, or even lessen the probability, of visible results. If you seek "the Kingdom of God, and his righteousness" first, according to Jesus, things needed in the world "shall be added unto you."[2]

Civility is not without breadth and balance. As the true political art, it synthesizes solitude, communication, and action. It also harmonizes public and private life.

CIVILITY AND PRIVATE LIFE

The practice of civility requires one to inhabit the public world. It means openness to all of human life, to all serious concerns of human beings everywhere. Hence Socrates spent his days in the gymnasia and agora. And as an effort at responsibility in action, civility involves one in politics, the master form of action. However, civility does not imply indifference to the private realm. Indeed, it is rooted, and may even be practiced, in that realm.

The link between civility and privacy consists partly in the conditions required by solitary communality. Privacy protects both solitude and communication. We misunderstand the relationship between the public and the private if we suppose that every act takes place in one sphere of life and not in the other. Many acts, such as political conversation among close friends, belong indistinguishably to public and private life. Civility, thus, is not practiced alone in parliaments and other public gatherings. As solitary communality it is practiced also in private. If it were not, if the habits, skills, and faith on which it depends were not cultivated within groupings shaped and restricted according to preferences and judgments of the participants, it could hardly survive.

The link between civility and privacy consists also in the dependence of civility on personal love. Civility cannot amount to much morally in someone incapable of personal love. The criticisms commonly levied against those who love humankind, but love no particular human being, are valid. This is not so much because loving humankind apart from particular persons is reprehensible as because it is impossible. Humankind is an abstraction; it is real only in the form of concrete and particular human beings. Love for humanity at large on the part of someone incapable of loving it in its singularity must be pretense or illusion. Hence the necessity of privacy. Civility must care for the private realm in which personal love has room to be realized. It cares in this way for its own source.

For a balanced understanding of the relations between civility and privacy, however, it must be noted that personal love is not primal and independent in relation to civility. It might seem that if one had to choose between civility without personal love and personal love without civility, that the latter would be seen to have immeasurably greater value. But this is an oversimplification. Personal love affirms the destiny of the one who is loved, and since that destiny is human and not exclusively individual, personal love is characterized by universality. But universality that is fully conscious and deliberately cultivated is civility. This indicates that personal love without civility is as unreal as civility without personal love. Common experience confirms this conclusion. It shows us that an intimate personal relationship may be based on a common interest in the cultural and political activities that constitute public life. It shows us too that a personal relationship excluding such an interest would be suspect; one might surmise that it rested on nothing but sensuality or some other impermanent and stultifying base. In a word, uncivil personal love would be—sensually or in some other way—a denial of destiny, a delusory love.

Civility may be said to be the form of full personal love, of love that is receptive to destiny in others. Civility makes conscious and explicit the universality inherent in personal love. This implies that complete absorption in a personal relationship, with public life ignored or denied, is destructive of the personal relationship itself. It is deprived of its essential universality. On the other hand, to say that civility is the form of full personal love underscores the constitutionalist, antitotalitarian character of civility. Obliviousness of private life, indifference toward concrete persons, must undermine civility.

These considerations may help to prepare us for seeing that civility, the true political art, is connected with the ultimate issues of human existence.

CIVILITY AND DESTINY

Civility rests on a certain attitude toward death. The theme of death so far has entered into this essay in two forms: first, in connection with humanity's efforts to master nature. Death is suffered in spite of all such efforts, and this discloses definitively their failure. Death has entered into this essay, second, in connection with efforts to master history: death is not only suffered but is inflicted in the nihilistic fury that may be provoked by the ironic consequences of humanity's struggle to enact its ideals. We now encounter the theme of death for the third time. Civility is not a stance designed to ward off death; it may, as the destiny of Socrates shows, expose one to death. The true political art is premised on a willingness to die.

In this way, however, death may be overcome. Civility is a state of openness to the mystery that one's life—one's destiny—may be lost in trying to save it and saved by allowing it to be lost. That which one holds to in trying to render life pleasurable and secure is not destiny but an existence that is doomed, regardless of all care and precautions, by biological laws. Letting go of the biological, hence dying, self, one may discover another self, the destined self. This is only to restate the irony of fate and destiny.

Modern society urges us continually, from all sides, to save our lives. Both business executives and politicians fulfill their ambitions by promising secure and pleasurable lives. We are induced to assert ourselves as dying beings. Hence the anomaly of modern society, pleasure-loving and ostensibly care-free, yet preoccupied with death. Anyone practicing the true political art is bound to resist the prevailing concentration on physical life and to try to remember that one's own life is vulnerable and insecure. But such weakness may turn out to be paradoxical, like the weakness of Paul, who said, "When I am weak, then am I strong."[3]

Civility rests on a certain attitude not only toward death but toward wrongdoing as well. It presupposes an acknowledgement of guilt. As I tried to show in chapter 1, no members of society are free of responsibility for the misdeeds of their people and rulers, although the nature and degree of the responsibility varies from individual to individual. It is true that civility means trying to maintain moral independence in political situations. But it also means remembering one's own fallibility—a fallibility rooted partly in the susceptibility of an immanent being to social determinism. And beyond the influence of society there is one's own urge toward self-exaltation and self-abandonment. In theological terms, civility is not an effort to win justification through works.

In the practice of civility, therefore, one looks toward transcendence not only for destiny in the form of life experienced in spite of death but also for destiny in the form of forgiveness. The dependence of destiny on divine mercy is explicitly recognized in the Bible. There may be a corresponding natural experience: that of sensing, either in the case of another or of oneself, that in spite of a life-record which is objectively dubious or unacceptable, a human being may be mysteriously justified.

To give up the dying and guilty self and to discover the destined self is to be reborn. Modern man has sought to gain life and innocence through revolution. He has tried in this way to be reborn through an act of political will. The practice of the true political art does not mean refusing, regardless of circumstances, even to consider revolution. But it does mean thinking of revolution as, in the words of the highly civil Locke, "an appeal to heaven"—an act undertaken in hope and not in willful assurance. And it means looking for one's true being as a gift of transcendence, not a collective enactment.

Civility is in essence living within historical time. Fate is a derangement of historical time, and it has its source in the ambition to rise above and master the flow of events in which our lives are set. Prevailing attitudes toward order reflect that ambition. Many become virtual inhabitants of an imagined order. If a good order does not now exist in actuality, it does in prospect and by their knowledge of what it is and how it is to be attained, as well as by their association with institutions and forces promoting its advent, they are lifted above history. But this of course only seems to be so, since human beings cannot actually dominate historical time. Hence events contradict intentions. Time takes the form of fate. Civility means resisting the urge to historical mastery and accepting with utmost lucidity one's essential temporality. It means entering in this way deliberately into historical time. The motive is simply to be accessible to one's destiny.

Certainly the survival of individuals in their full humanity will often be determined by their capacity for standing out against the incivility of their times. Perhaps the survival of civilization may depend on such individuals—a saving remnant who will accept the responsibilities implicit in the true political art.

This art depends ultimately on one's capacity for a certain kind of love—independent and inquiring, politically sensitive. "Because iniquity shall abound," Jesus said, looking toward the upheavals in which he expected history to end, "the love of many shall wax cold."[4] Almost everyone today has experienced how readily love—attentiveness toward human beings, openness toward transcendence—"waxes cold." Jesus added, however, that "he that shall endure unto the end, the same shall be saved." It may be said that civility is what is meant, in political terms, by enduring unto the end. Perhaps we may understand the true political art as resisting fate through love, waiting for the destiny that singles out individuals and, even when they are killed by fate, saves them from fate.

NOTES

1. Fate

1. Reinhold Niebuhr, *The Irony of American History* (New York: Charles Scribner's Sons, 1952), p. viii.
2. Feodor Dostoevsky, *Crime and Punishment*, trans. Jessie Coulson (New York: W. W. Norton & Co., 1964), p. 67.
3. Jonathan Schell, *The Time of Illusion* (New York: Alfred A. Knopf, 1976), p. 6 (italics added).
4. Romans 5:3 (Revised Standard Version).
5. Boris Pasternak, *Doctor Zhivago* (New York: Pantheon, 1958), p. 500.

2. Destiny

1. Matthew 11:16 (King James translation).
2. John 8:32 (King James translation).
3. Ernest Hemingway, *For Whom the Bell Tolls* (New York: Charles Scribner's Sons, 1940), p. 387.
4. Carl Sandburg, *Abraham Lincoln: The War Years* (New York: Harcourt, Brace & Co., 1939), III, 663.

3. Man against Nature

1. These phrases are found, respectively, in Psalms 24:1, 36:5, 36:6 and 77:19 (King James translation).
2. Job 12:8 (King James translation).
3. Alfred Zimmern, *The Greek Commonwealth: Politics and Economics in Fifth-Century Athens*, 5th ed., rev. (London: Oxford University Press, 1931), p. 68.
4. Bernard Berenson, *The Italian Painters of the Renaissance* (London: Oxford University Press, n.d.).

5. Genesis 3:19 (King James translation).

6. Romans 8:21-22 (King James translation).

7. Karl Marx, *Economic and Philosophical Manuscripts*, trans. T. B. Bottomore, in Erich Fromm, *Marx's Concept of Man* (New York: Frederick Ungar Publishing Co., 1961), pp. 135 and 129 respectively.

8. Robert Jay Lifton, *Revolutionary Immortality: Mao Tse-tung and the Chinese Cultural Revolution* (New York: Vintage Books, 1968).

4. Man against Humanity

1. Martin Buber, *I and Thou*, 2nd ed., trans. Ronald Gregor Smith (New York: Charles Scribner's Sons, 1958), p. 9.

5. The Fury of History

1. Genesis 3:22 (Revised Standard Version).

2. Romans 8:28 (King James translation).

3. Richard Harris, *Death of a Revolutionary: Che Guevara's Last Mission* (New York: Collier Books, 1970), p. 118.

4. The phrase is the subtitle and theme of Laski's *The Rise of Liberalism: The Philosophy of a Business Civilization* (New York: Harper & Row, 1936).

5. Psalm 115:16 (King James translation).

6. John Locke, *Two Treatises of Government*, ed. Peter Laslett (Cambridge: University Press, 1960), p. 304.

7. Herman Melville, *Moby-Dick or, The Whale*, ed. Luther S. Mansfield and Howard P. Vincent (New York: Hendricks House, 1952), pp. 512 and 162 respectively.

8. Ibid., p. 536.

9. Ibid.

6. The True Political Art

1. Franz Kafka, *The Trial*, trans. Willa and Edwin Muir (New York: Schocken Books, 1968), p. 225.

2. Matthew 6:33 (King James translation).

3. II Corinthians 12:10 (King James translation).

4. Matthew 24:12-13 (King James translation).

INDEX

Adam, 49, 73, 120
Aristotle, 65
Augustine, 48, 65, 123, 147, 153, 157

Becket, Thomas à, 51
Beethoven, Ludwig von, 65
Bergson, Henri, 41, 96
Bonhoeffer, Dietrich, 56
Bosanquet, Bernard, 55
Boswell, James, 123
Burke, Edmund, 126

Caesar, Julius, 50
Cezanne, Paul, 16
Christ, see Jesus Christ

da Vinci, Leonardo, 50
Dostoevsky, Fëdor, 18-19, 22, 31, 51, 57, 85-87, 142

Epicurus, 145-148

Freud, Sigmund, 11-12, 33, 52-53, 124

Guevara, Che, 128

Hemingway, Ernest, 55-56
Hitler, Adolph, 18, 56, 87, 141-143, 162

Jesus Christ, 7, 25, 41, 45-46, 49-51, 58, 89, 121, 168
Job, 69, 139
John the Evangelist, 54, 58, 65

Kafka, Franz, 158
Kant, Immanuel, 1, 19, 44, 48, 66, 121
Kennedy, John F., 32
Kierkegaard, Sören, 2, 147

Laski, Harold, 130
Lawrence, D. H., 30
Lenin, Vladimir, 28, 42, 97
Lincoln, Abraham, 12, 35, 57-58, 156
Locke, John, 136, 138, 168
Luther, Martin, 32, 56

Mao Tse-tung, 87
Marcus Aurelius (Antoninus), 119
Marcuse, Herbert, 73
Marx, Karl, 11-12, 33, 42, 45, 52-53, 73-74, 82-83, 91, 109-110, 124, 133-134, 137
Matisse, Henri, 65
Melville, Herman, 143-144
Mill, John Stuart, 38

Nietzsche, Friedrich, 141, 143